Garway Hill
through the Ages

This book is dedicated to the memory of
Doreen Ruck of Garway Hill,
Teacher and Local Historian
1927-2007

Garway Hill through the Ages

Compiled and Edited by
Joan and Brian Thomas

Logaston Press

LOGASTON PRESS
Little Logaston Woonton Almeley
Herefordshire HR3 6QH
logastonpress.co.uk

First published by Logaston Press 2007
Copyright © Author of each chapter 2007

ISBN 978 1904396 88 8

Set in Times by Logaston Press
and printed in Great Britain by
Cromwell Press Ltd, Trowbridge

Contents

Garway Hill

Can there be a hill more fair
A finer place to stand and stare
At the finest views that man can find
To the mountains of Wales that still the mind
The Monnow river flowing slowly by
The Graig gradually rising up against the sky.

Oh what the sights this hill has seen
Stories of what and might have been
From Stone Age Men and Celts in Woad
The Roman Legions' fort and road
Saxons, Vikings, Normans take their turn
To rob and kill and house to burn.

On Garway Hill glowed shining beacons
Sending signals for whatever reasons
Warning folk of marauders movements
Heralding news of great achievements.
Power in the hands of the great and the good
Controlling the people as they most surely would.

The sun descends behind the hill
And daylight fades and all is still.
 Darkness brings to a close another day
Nocturnal creatures now hold sway
The barking fox, the wise old owl,
Birds are silent and animals prowl.

All too soon the night has gone
A new day dawns, the moon has shone
Morning shadows from the sun are cast
 On gorse and bracken growing fast.
Grazing animals from their rest arise
As Garway Hill becomes alive.

Brian Thomas

Foreword

The invitation to write the foreword to this book has in many ways strengthened my family's ties with the Parish of Garway. My brother and I are proud of our association with Garway Hill and other local Common Land. This connection dates from our Grandfather Ernest Lawley who acquired the Lordship of the Manor in 1920. Perhaps it was the romance of Garway Hill that led to Dennis de Labillière and Kitty Lawley meeting, falling in love and marrying. Dennis was the second son of the Reverend Edgar de Labillière, who, after the First World War was the vicar of nearby Llangattock, while Kitty was second daughter of Arthur Lawley the owner of Hilston Park and the Lord of the Manor of Garway. Thus my brothers and myself came into being.

From Prehistoric times to the present day Garway Hill has hidden its history, much of it undiscovered until the past decade. This enchanting book, painstakingly put together by dedicated local authors lead by Joan Fleming-Yates, brings it all to life and provides an important landmark and record for future generations.

These chapters are a tribute to the human endeavour that has marked the often harsh events that this prominent hill and its people have experienced over the ages. This history culminated with culminating with the disastrously mismanaged foot and mouth outbreak in 2001 when all the live stock had to be destroyed and the hill reverted to a bracken desert. Only now, six years later, it is coming under control thanks to the efforts of a diligent team of commoners.

Modern satellite technology gave archaeologists and local researchers the opportunity, eagerly grasped, to identify and subsequently uncover the farmstead forts of the Iron Age dating back more than 2000 years.

During the middle ages the farming community were barely able to provide sufficient food for the crowded population of Herefordshire and much of the upper common land was derogated to provide back up strip and terrace plots to help increase the county's food producing area. The unimaginable horror of the Black Death which swept England in 1345 corrected this imbalance with a vicious decimation of the county's population and Garway Hill, with the poor soil no longer required for food production, reverted to its historical role and became waste land once again.

Perhaps the most enchanting comments come in the all too short Chapter describing the flora and fauna of Garway Hill. It provides a habitat for the great crested newt and for the increasingly rare mud snail. The great flood in 1959 caused water to sweep off the hill destroying property, buildings and almost human life in the foothills. It reminds us that such extreme conditions are not reserved to the global warming of the present day.

My surviving brother David Bennetts and I, along with the sons of my deceased brother Michael, are proud to have inherited the Title Lord of the Manor of Garway.

We shall guard our heritage with pride.

Peter de la Billière

Peter de la Billière

Acknowledgements

The successful completion of a book such as this inevitably involves the co-operation of the local community both from Garway and the neighbouring parishes who were willing to talk to us, recalling what were sometimes hazy memories of days gone by.

With so many people involved it would be unfair to single out individuals for their specific help and unwise to attempt to mention them all by name for fear of missing someone out. Therefore we would like to express our gratitude to everyone who in any way contributed to the production of this book.

Introduction

This book has its origins in the foot and mouth disease epidemic which ravaged the area during the Spring of 2001. Hazy ideas have a wonderful habit of evolving into something worthwhile and I hope that this is no exception.

Following the rounding up and culling of the hill's entire sheep population, nature once again took over. The invasive bracken went unchecked making it difficult to even walk over the common. This prompted two local ladies to declare, 'something must be done'. Their resolve led to the setting up of a Commoners Association with the aim of managing the common in the future. At the AGM of the Commoners Association in May 2005, the Herefordshire Nature Trust gave a presentation about the Community Commons Project, which involves twelve Herefordshire commons. A motion was agreed that the Garway Hill Commoners Association should formally support the Community Commons Project in relation to Garway Hill. Herefordshire Nature Trust and other wildlife organisations have since been invited to become involved. An approach was made to Dr Neil Rimmington, the Countryside Adviser for Archaeology, who was best positioned to advise on how to proceed with a project orientated towards the investigation of the history and archaeology of the common from early times up to the present day.

In due course a programme was put in place which would lead to the recording of the archaeological features, especially the earthwork enclosure. A detailed survey followed by a small scale-excavation of the site was to take place. A grant from the Local Heritage Initiative was secured, part of which was to help finance the publication of this book and the setting up of a website.

Two small committees of volunteers were assembled, one for the website and one for the book. The members of the book committee each agreed to write a chapter. After several meetings spread over the winter months of 2006/7, where much discussion took place and numerous glasses of wine consumed, the book was ready for publication. Most of the contributors had no previous experience of writing about local history but they set to — with great enthusiasm. They talked to the locals, trawled through the Hereford County Record Office and helped with the archaeology. A 'memories' day led to contacts with people who live on Garway Hill, some of them for all of their lives, and whose reminiscences have added colour to the overall picture. Of necessity, we have wandered away from the common on the summit of Garway Hill because it is the people whose families, for generations, have settled all around the hill who make the story come alive. Although the common itself lies in the parish and Manor of Garway, many of the dwellings are in Orcop and Kentchurch.

As for the earthwork enclosure, this has long been the subject of much speculation but in reality it remained an enigma. Mr Richard Kay carried out a detailed study of the site in 1967 but did not excavate it. His finds were recorded in the *Woolhope Club Transactions* (Vol XXX1X 1967). Theories ranged from it being a prehistoric site, a Roman fortlet to a medieval farmstead. We were there to find the answers.

The archaeological dig, which took place in June 2006 during a heat wave, proved to be a huge local attraction with numerous visitors and helpers. Hopefully, we now have answers to most of the questions which must surely have puzzled men with inquiring minds for the past two thousand years.

1 Early Settlements

Stone Age to Bronze Age

During the Ice Age Britain was part of the landmass we know as the continent. Animals wandered freely, closely followed by nomadic hunters in their never ending search for food. Eventually the climate improved and as the ice melted Britain became separated from the rest of Europe to become an insular home for animals and the people who pursued them. The early hunters had no knowledge of metal, their only weapons were those they made from materials readily available: stone, wood and bone. Tools from wood and bone have long since decomposed and the earliest stone tools often cannot be easily identified from amongst naturally shaped pieces of rock. However, it is clear that prehistoric people were inventive and eventually they discovered that certain stones such as flint could be flaked and trimmed into shape. This important step in history has enabled archaeologists to recognise and date Stone Age tools and weapons. As flint does not occur naturally in Herefordshire any flint implements found in and around Garway were certainly brought here by our Stone Age ancestors.

Archaeologists have found that when fields are ploughed, flints of varying age and type are brought to the surface. In the 1980s children of Garway School were given permission to 'walk' a ploughed field alongside the River Monnow on Demesne Farm. Among their finds were flints from each of the three Stone Ages, Palaeolithic (Early) up to 10,000BC; Mesolithic (Middle) 10,000 – 4,500BC and Neolithic (Late or 'New') 4,500 – 2,300BC. Some of these flints were waste fragments that had fallen while the weapon or tool was being fashioned and some were burnt. Both facts suggest time spent in the area if only for a day or two and give proof that the route along the Monnow Valley has been continuously used from time immemorial. Sue Rice who lives locally has become interested in, and expert at, field walking. Her finds prove once again that history is all around us and a lot of it under our feet. She has found pieces of worked flint, scrapers and blades from the Middle Stone Age and worked flint scrapers, blades, arrowheads and knives from the Late Stone Age, all of these and many more were found in and around Garway and Orcop.

Armed with only their handmade weapons the Stone Age hunters would lie in wait for woolly mammoth, woolly rhinoceros, red deer, wild ox or wild pig. The meat these animals provided was essential to these prehistoric people but skin and fur, once scraped free of flesh with flint scrapers, made warm garments for them and even the bones had many uses. When pierced, smaller bones could be threaded with animal sinew and used to join pieces of fur or skin together, when sharpened they could hold clothes in place. Animal teeth and carved bone threaded together made desirable necklaces and bracelets, while the larger bones and antlers were ready made weapons and tools.

During the thousands of years that separated the Palaeolithic and Neolithic people, a way of life developed in which animals were domesticated and crops grown. Gone was the nomadic, hunting life and decamping was only necessary when fresh pasture was needed for the animals. Hunters and gatherers had become farmers and herders. Once living in a settled area they became more aware of what was in the ground around them. Clay was found and potters were added to the workforce of the community. When metals were found their qualities were soon exploited. Copper, tin, gold and silver were found to be in rocks that didn't flake when struck but were soft enough to be shaped. Gold and silver were too soft to be of any utilitarian use but copper and tin were soon being used to make weapons and tools. We will never know exactly how the melting effect of heat upon these metals was realized but it was, probably by accident when some fell into a fire. Next it was found that when metal cooled it assumed the shape of any hollow it dropped into and soon pottery moulds were being used to form a whole range of articles. An even greater discovery came about when tin and copper were used together to form bronze, a strong alloy which was much harder than either metal on its own. It was around 2,300BC when the Bronze Age is considered to have commenced and among finds made on Garway Hill was a piece of Bronze Age pottery. Bronze gradually replaced stone in the making of weapons and tools while gold and silver continued to be made into delicate and intricately designed jewellery.

People of the Iron Age

The process of iron-making was discovered about 1,300BC by Hittites, the people of modern day Turkey. They managed to keep it their secret while at the same time letting it be known that the superb weapons they were making with this wondrous metal were stronger than anything known and it was about 500 years before the new process reached Britain. Clearwell Caves in the Forest of Dean have been used as a source of iron ore since the 5th century BC where the ore was readily dug at the surface. Once the surface deposits had been used up miners entered the natural cave system to dig out the ore encrusted in the walls.

Bronze could not compete with iron for strength but it continued to be used along with silver and gold for jewellery and ornamentation. Iron eventually replaced bronze in agricultural tools, making for easier planting and harvesting of crops and enabling a more settled way of life.

The people of the Iron Age became known as Celts from *Keltoi,* the name given to them by contemporary Greek writers. Greek and Roman writers recorded much about the Celts and their possessions, noting especially their long moustaches and trousers, and noted that some fought wearing only body-paint.

Celts, highly organised groups of people, lived in or close to settlements known as hillforts. Each site was enclosed by a strong rampart with an adjacent deep ditch, and a guarded entrance which could be safely secured at dusk. Herefordshire has an abundance of hillfort sites but they do not conform to a standard size. The largest is at Credenhill which has an internal area of 49 acres while others vary from 26 acres at Sutton Walls to one acre at Dorstone. Recently aerial photographs were taken of a site above Skenfrith, it was then walked and is now being considered as a probable hillfort. Food is and always has been of paramount importance to man and all the hillforts appear to have been surrounded by small farmsteads where Celtic families lived and produced food crops. The 2007 Garway Hill dig revealed evidence of a small Iron Age settlement complete with rampart, ditch, a round house and pieces of pottery.

The Celts were excellent farmers who grew wheat, barley, oats, rye, peas and beans. They kept a large variety of domesticated animals including dogs. Huge wolfhound types were ideal hunting dogs; smaller breeds were useful for herding and very small dogs were kept as pets. A small breed of sheep, similar to the Soay sheep found in the Outer Hebrides which lose their wool freely, were kept especially for their wool which could be plucked to be spun and woven into cloth. Sheep also provided milk, which was used to make butter and cheese, and meat which could be eaten fresh or salted and kept in large pottery containers until needed. Goats supplied more milk and meat and also goatskin which was made into clothing. The Celts found out how to use horses to the greatest advantage not only for riding but by harnessing them to chariots for battle and to carts for farm work. The most beautifully decorated horse harnesses have been found with burial goods of important men and women. Cattle too were used to pull carts but also provided milk, butter, cheese, meat and hides, even their horns were used as drinking vessels. Pork was considered the choicest meat of all and pigskin made superior garments. Excavation sites have revealed bones and eggshells which could have come from domesticated, or wild, fowl. Woodland adjacent to the hillforts would have been home to a variety of wild animals large and small. Bears, deer, wolves, rabbits, stoats and weasels would all have been hunted for their skins and many made good eating as did birds and fish. Wild bees provided sweet honey which was not only a delicious treat but when fermented was used to make mead, a special drink of the Celts which they kept for important feasts. Barley was used in the brewing of ale, another favourite and more plentiful drink. In the autumn woodland trees produced a bounty of nuts — the people enjoyed chestnuts and hazelnuts while their pigs were taken out to feast on acorns and beechmast.

The men and women of the Iron Age were splendid craftsmen, their skill in spinning, weaving and dyeing ensured warm, colourful clothing while the smiths' expertise gave them superb weapons for defence or attack, excellent tools for building and farming plus exquisite jewellery with which to enrich their lives. Their handcrafted items, including pottery and basketwork of an equally high standard, were everyday essentials for the Celts.

The Celts inhabited a huge area of Europe reaching as far west as Ireland and possibly as far east as China. Mummified bodies, whose clothing and physical attributes fit perfectly with the Greeks' recorded description of the Keltoi, have been found perfectly preserved in the salty sand of the Chinese desert. One was an infant and wrapped up with it was a 3,000 year old state-of-the-art baby feeder made from the udder of a sheep complete with a nipple, another example of the ingenuity of the people of the Iron Age.

Map showing the location of the tribes of Britain at the time of the Roman invasion

From the writings of the Greek and Roman historians we learn that the Celts loved nothing better than to find an excuse for combat, they wore breastplates and helmets, fought with long swords and javelins, were excellent horsemen and could fight from chariots. Actual proof of these details has been found in Celtic burials containing all the necessities for the journey to the Otherworld and for the life there afterwards. The Celts firmly believed in an afterlife in the home of the gods, the Otherworld was not looked upon with fear but rather as the ultimate goal. Celtic chiefs have been found buried with their chariots, horses, slaves, weapons and armour ready to fight in the next life. Both men and women loved personal decoration and many brooches, rings, bracelets, anklets, necklaces, beads and belts all made from bronze, gold or silver have been found in their owners' graves. In Gloucester Museum is a fine bronze mirror which was found among other pieces of jewellery with a female skeleton in Birdlip, Gloucestershire, in 1879.

During the Iron Age tribes of varying size, power and wealth occupied the British Isles, and a sophisticated civilization had developed with a powerful and well-organised society. The tribes of south-east Britain were the strongest and most prosperous, their territory included large areas of coastline and owning the ports gave them control over trade with the continent. These were the people who encountered Julius Caesar and bargained with him.

Roman Invasion

After successfully adding Gaul to the ever-growing Roman Empire Julius Caesar turned his attention to Britain. In 55BC he made a tentative reconnaissance of the island and followed it up a year later with an unsuccessful attempt at conquest. However these forays into the south-east of Britain resulted in the surrender of local tribes. One of them, the powerful Catuvellauni, would unexpectedly provide a positive link with the Welsh Marches. Before Caesar left Britain to quell a revolt in Gaul he had agreed terms with leaders of the defeated tribes. Britain would export gold, silver, slaves, hunting dogs, grain, cattle, iron and hides to the Roman Army on the continent in return for ivory, glass, amber, wine, pottery and oil.

For the next century, through the reigns of Augustus, Tiberius and Caligula, Britain was left alone, and Britain's trade grew. The Catuvellauni prospered and increased their territory until they dominated almost the whole of south-east Britain which gave them absolute control over the trade routes. Cunobelin, leader of the Catuvellauni, died in 41AD and was succeeded by his sons Togodumnus and Caratacus.

In 43AD the Roman Emperor Claudius decided that Britain should become part of the Roman Empire. By this time Gaul was a fully organised Roman province, complete with permanent camps and a superior fighting force, an excellent base from which to begin an assault. Claudius gave command of the invasion to Aulus Plautius, an experienced and formidable leader who landed with more than 40,000 men near Richborough. He soon encountered the armies of Togodumnus and Caratacus who were both defeated in separate battles. The Britons retreated and regrouped only to be routed again. Togodumnus was killed and Caratacus fled to the west. Unfortunately there is a gap in the historians' records of the Roman Invasion of Britain, we can only guess where Caratacus was during this period but can be sure that the Romans were well aware of his presence.

By 47AD most of south-east and central Britain was covered by a network of Roman roads interspersed with forts and Aulus Plautius returned to Rome where he was publicly acknowledged as a conquering hero. His successor as Governor of Britain was Ostorius Scapula, a ruthless leader whose first action was to disarm the British leaders who had given allegiance to the invading Romans. Scapula then proceeded westwards to gain control of the unconquered tribes of the borderlands. Those he did not subdue fled before his army into the hills. Caratacus was one of those driven west into the mountains of Wales where his charisma and military skill ensured an enthusiastic welcome from the local tribes. The southern area of the Welsh Marches was home country to the Silures and as well as providing strongholds in the safety of the mountains where they could virtually disappear, gave access into, and out from, Roman held territory along the valleys of the Severn, Wye and Monnow. Using guerrilla tactics the Silures and Caratacus fought and won many battles against Scapula and his Roman Army. Their success gave them greater resolution but unfortunately it had a similar effect upon Ostorius Scapula who was so incensed by these undaunted natives that he threatened to exterminate them.

It was obvious that Ostorius Scapula, with his tremendous reserves, a thoroughly

A Roman legionary
(drawn by Marc Rice)

professional army and a personal determination to exterminate the guerrilla fighters, would eventually succeed and so Caratacus and the Silures moved north to join up with the Ordovices. The *Red Book of Gwent* tells that 'the men of Britain, from the prince to the slave became his [Caratacus] followers' and Tacitus wrote how 'Caratacus was joined by everyone who feared a Roman peace'. In 51AD Caratacus chose the site for the final confrontation with the Roman Army, a site which to this day has not been positively identified. Tacitus describes how 'Caratacus, as he hastened to one point and another, stressed that this was the day, this the battle, which would either win back their freedom or enslave them for ever. His exhortations were applauded. Then every man swore by his tribal oath that no enemy weapons would make them yield — and no wounds either.' The Celts responded to his words by putting up a tremendous fight but they were no match for the Roman Army. Caratacus escaped to find safety with Cartimandua, Queen of the Brigantes, but she betrayed him and handed him over to the Romans. Caratacus' reputation had spread to Rome and he and his family were taken there to be displayed to the citizens and their Emperor Claudius. Caratucus was not intimidated by the city or its people and made a speech in which he is said to have asked, 'Why do you, with all these great possessions, still covet our poor huts?' Caratacus has become known in Welsh history as Caradoc, a great Welsh hero.

Caplar Camp and Caplar Wood near Fownhope, and Oyster Hill near Ledbury possibly derive from the name Ostorius Scapula and so give proof to his presence in Herefordshire, Recorded in folklore is the slaughter on Great Doward at Whitchurch near

Site of the Roman fort excavated in 1986 at Castlefield Farm
by Monmouth Archaeological Society (Joan Fleming-Yates)

Monmouth when, 'Bodies of British and Romans were tumbled into the river after the legions had taken the Silurian fort on the hilltop and the river ran red with their blood'.

In the early 1980s members of Monmouth Archaeological Society walked a field just west of Garway and were thrilled to find fragments of Samian ware. This red pottery was used throughout the Roman Empire for 400 years and has become accepted as a positive indication of Roman occupation. With the farmer's permission an archaeological dig took place in the area in 1986, when evidence was uncovered of a timber-built, 1st-century AD, Roman fort. It had been strategically placed to hold and guard the Monnow Valley between Roman held territory and the Silures. Archaeological evidence was found from two phases of occupation and included pottery sherds and coins from the Emperors Gaius 37-41AD, his nickname was Caligula — Little Boots; Nero 54-68AD and Vespasian 69-79AD. Roman military tactics included the building of forts a day's march apart which were placed to control important routes, river crossings and native settlements. The late Dr. Graham Webster, an authority on the Roman Army, had always expected a fort to be found in the area, but probably at Grosmont. He was delighted when he visited the dig and realised just how close this fort was to his original estimate.

In his book *The Roman Imperial Army* Dr. Webster describes the three different army sites that are often acknowledged under the words camp or fort. The smallest were Marching Camps, which were just that, used by soldiers who were away from their permanent barracks while out on campaign. The largest were Legionary Fortresses, the main bases of the occupying forces who were ready to be deployed when and wherever necessary. The fort discovered in the Monnow Valley was a Permanent Fort, similar to but not as big as a Legionary Fortress. In the first century AD Permanent Forts were specifically chosen bases from which troops could be sent out to deal with local problems. Tacitus tells how Roman troops were building a fort somewhere in Silurian territory when they were suddenly surrounded and only saved when help came from a nearby fortress. Even so the casualties included the chief of staff and eight company commanders. The Roman soldiers who built the fort close to Garway in the Monnow Valley would have had a similarly dangerous task being so close to the hills that gave security to the guerrilla forces.

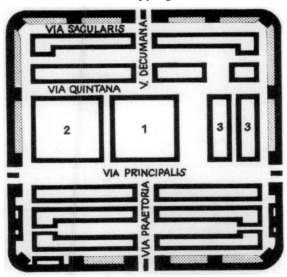

A typical Roman fort plan with division into three parts: a central rage with HQ (1), the commandant's house (2) and granaries (3), and a front portion (bottom third) and rear portion with barracks, stores and other buildings.
(© Tasamine Cole)

The Roman fort west of Garway would have conformed to a regulation pattern, now commonly known as

7

'playing card shape' — rectangular with rounded corners. Surrounded by huge ditches topped with massive ramparts the fort had four entrances, one sited centrally on each side, complete with gatehouses where traffic could be controlled in and out. Streets laid with precision by army surveyors became crossroads at the centre of the fort and this was where the HQ stood housing the administration offices, along with a great hall used for ceremonial and official occasions. A regimental shrine, barracks, latrines, wash-houses, a hospital, granaries, ovens and cookhouses were always standard requirements. Baths played an important part in Roman life, civil and military, and were usually sited outside a fort. It is hard to imagine such an impressive Roman fort existing alongside the road linking Garway and Pontrilas but it gives proof to the importance of such a route along the river valley in the first century AD. Further archaeological evidence showed that the fort had been burned; this could have been done by the Romans themselves not wanting to leave a fortified site for the enemy, or maybe the fort was destroyed by that very enemy. On their field walk, which was further east of the site, the children of Garway School had found pieces of iron slag and a piece of furnace lining which were certainly Roman as any later furnaces would not have been sited so far out into the countryside.

Ramping House is about halfway between Demesne Farm and Castlefield Farm. In his book *English Field Names* John Field writes that 'rampart' was a name given to land beside a causeway or part of a Roman road. The Romans are famous for their straight roads and between Ramping House and the site of the fort the road is unusually straight for a country road otherwise full of bends. The field on the opposite side of the road to Ramping House is named Ford Meadow, obviously the Monnow is shallow enough to ford here. Immediately west of Ramping House is a very well preserved spring and imagination could allow us to visualize the Roman army making offerings at this very spring, entreating the gods to protect them on their venture, or offering thanks for their safe return.

The Roman occupation of Britain lasted for about 400 years and during that time the Romans completely organised and dominated the people they had conquered. But early in the fourth century they were forced to return to Italy to protect Rome from Germanic invaders, the Visigoths. With the departure of the Roman Army the way was open to invaders from northern Europe — Angles, Saxons and Jutes — and soon the greater part of Britain became England, land of the Angles.

The Age of Saints

By the time the Romans left Britain Christianity was just becoming known and accepted in Europe. It is said that sometime before he became pope, Gregory had seen some blond haired boys in the slave market in Rome and when told they were Angles from Britain he replied that they were surely 'non Angli sed angeli' — not Angles but angels. He then declared that it was especially important for such people to be converted to the Christian faith and that he should lead a group of missionaries. Unfortunately for Gregory he was kept too busy to accomplish his desire but he never forgot the 'angels'. When he became pope he chose Augustine to convert the Angles and in 597 Augustine and 40 monks landed in Kent to begin their missionary work.

In today's Cornwall, Wales, Scotland and the north of England the new religion was already being spread by Celtic monks. Celts had fled north and west from the Roman Army and the early years of the Anglo-Saxon invasion did nothing to encourage them out from their strongholds. It was here that Celtic Christianity developed but with differences, one was the remoteness from Rome and therefore lack of instruction from the pope and another was the language. Isolation, which had been partly self-imposed by the Celts themselves had strengthened their own language, and it has been said that the Celtic language could be understood throughout the land from Cornwall to Scotland. By the time Augustine arrived in England the abbots and monks of the Celtic Church had spread their message over a huge area. Through their tireless enthusiasm and total commitment they became known as Saints and the period in which they lived, the Age of Saints. The fact that they had no direct contact with the leaders of the Roman Church, who were constantly making decisions on the structure of the new religion did not deter them in the least. They were confidant in the work they were doing and assured by their obvious success.

At this time Garway was in the kingdom of Archenfield, an area bounded by the Rivers Dore, Wye and Monnow. One of the earliest Welsh Saints is believed to have been the grandson of the King of Archenfield; his name was Dyfrig and he was born in Madley around 450AD. His name becomes Dubricius in Latin and Devereux in French and local churches have been dedicated to him at Ballingham, Hentland, St. Devereux (near Wormbridge) and Whitchurch. Dyfrig founded several monasteries in Archenfield, the most well known was at Llanfrother in Hentland, originally *Hen Llan* meaning Old Church. Dyfrig is even mentioned in Geoffrey of Monmouth's book *History of the Kings of England*: 'Dubricius lamented the sad state of his country. He called other bishops to him and bestowed the crown of the kingdom upon Arthur'.

An entry in the Book of Llandaff gives evidence that early in the 6th century monasticism reached Garway. Page 62 records that:

> Guorvodu, King of the region of Ercycg [Archenfield], gave another piece of land, that is an uncia of land, for the sake of the heavenly kingdom, unto God and St. Dubricius and his community, and to his church of the south of the isle of Britain, and into the hands of Bishop Uvelbiu, and to all his successors who should enter upon that office, for ever, and with the whole liberty and all common in field and in woods, in water and in pastures. And walking around the piece of land, with the holy cross going on before, with the holy relics, and with sprinkling of holy water in the midst, he founded the place in honour of the Holy Trinity; and placed there Guorvoe, his priest, and commended the place to him, to serve for the permanent use of a church.

A list of witnesses, clergy and laity, follows.

This description of the consecration of the land in Garway is delightful. With the colourful procession, the Holy Cross, the relics and the ritual sprinkling of Holy Water it was surely an awesome sight for any local onlookers. Relics were precious possessions, eagerly acquired by all churches. They were the remains or possessions of saints or other religious men and women, and could be a phial of blood, a lock of hair or a fragment of clothing, but more often bones, not necessarily the whole skeleton but more often a finger, hand, tooth or foot. All were attributed with healing powers and the ability to protect both the church and the congregation. Relics were kept in highly decorated boxes known as reliquaries and were carried in procession on special occasions such as the dedication of the religious site in Garway.

A church was built on the land given by the King of Archenfield and it was a 'clas' church, home to a resident body of monks. Unfortunately there are no details of the actual location and the timber buildings have left no trace. But as we know that there has been a religious site in Garway for well over 1,400 years there is no reason to suppose that the same site has not been in continuous use for all that time. There is a spring in the south-east corner of the present churchyard and a ready water supply would be essential for everyday use by the members of the clas, and for the ceremony of baptism. Another important consideration was the proximity to the highway, as good roadways and tracks would be needed by the peripatetic monks and Garway's east-west and north-south roads would have met this requirement. Celibacy was not an issue in the clas and domestic buildings housed the missionary monks and their families. Lodgings for visitors and the sick would always be available as hospitality was an important facet of Celtic tradition. Stables, barns and workshops would be in evidence, in fact all the buildings necessary for self sufficiency would be found in the clas enclosure.

2 A History of Common Land

The Parish of Garway has the priceless asset of owning an enviable amount of common land. There are in fact four areas of common, the smallest being Blackhouse which is just opposite the road leading to Bagwyllydiart. This tiny common is now covered with brambles and scrub under which can be found the base of the old standing cross, the shaft of which is in Garway churchyard. There is common land at Broad Oak around the crossroads where once stood a round Toll House. The land which was used as a car park in front of the Broad Oak Inn was also common land. However, when the pub was closed and sold as a private house this area was enclosed. The ancient oak, which gave the hamlet its name, still stands in front of this ancient inn.

The 23 acres of common opposite the Garway Moon Inn are used mainly for recreation. There is an area which has been prepared for playing games and is kept mown during the summer months, alongside which is a children's playground. The rest of the common is natural grassland and woodland with an abundance of wildflowers, birds and other wildlife. On certain areas of the common the grass is cut for hay in the late summer after the wild flowers have set their seed.

The largest area of common land in the parish is, however, Garway Hill Common at over 200 acres and rising to a height of 1,206 feet. This area has always been a working common with the farmers and smallholders who live around the hill having common rights to graze their stock.

The title 'common' gives rise to a misconception; it implies common ownership with freedom to roam at will. However, common land is private land with certain people having rights over that land. The law as it applies to commons is complex and has changed recently under the Countryside and Rights of Way Act (2000). The Commons Registration Act (1965) led to the identification of 9,000 separate units of common land in England and Wales ranging from very small parcels to the great tracts of Dartmoor and Bodmin Moor and the fells of the Lake District and the mountains of Snowdonia. In all 1.3 million acres of common land was registered. Every sort of habitat is encountered from the Forest of Dean to the Welsh Mountains, from the heath lands of Surrey to the coast of Norfolk.

Common Land is private property and is owned by an individual or a corporation and has always been so since time immemorial. The owner of the common land is the Lord of the Manor in which the common lies, or his legal descendant or representative. One of the unique features of common land is the rights possessed by some people over the common.

These rights are restricted to just a few people and these days they are usually attached to a property. These rights are:

> The right of common pasture – the right to graze one's animals over the herbage.
> Estovers – the right to gather wood for fuel.
> Turbary – the right to dig turf for fuel or roofing.
> Piscary – the right to fish in common waters.
> The right to cut bracken for fuel or cattle-bedding.

No changes may be made to the common without the consent of the whole body of commoners. This right has had the effect of protecting commons from hasty and ill-considered change either by the Lord of the Manor or, more recently, ill-considered development. The owner, or anyone else, is discouraged by law from erecting any building upon common land, even the most modest fence, and is obliged to leave the land open. The effect of this law is to conserve areas, small or large, in the countryside where can be found completely natural grassland, unfenced and unploughed, giving some of our most distinctive scenery and wildlife.

There is no mention of common land as such before the Norman Conquest when much of the countryside was wild and ownerless. Agriculture was operated in a communal manner with the animals grazing on the land that was not being used for growing crops. W.G. Hoskins considered that the rights of common probably antedate the idea of private ownership of land, and are therefore of vast antiquity. It is unlikely that the Norman conquerors would have granted privileges to conquered people that they did not already possess. Thus, when King William I seized ownership of the whole country and gave or sold areas of it to his followers, he must have considered it wise to leave the customary rights in place. We know this happened locally, for the Domesday Book stated quite clearly that the Welsh in Archenfield (that area of country between the rivers Dore, Wye and Monnow) should keep their own customs and lists what these customs were.

Originally common land was common property. Today it is all private property subject to certain rights over its surface. The change in status was the result of the appropriation of land by new owners following the Norman Conquest. Large areas of land were absorbed into great estates or Manors that formed the new basis of the rural economy. By the year 1250 most commons, except perhaps the vast open tracts of land in the Welsh Mountains, belonged to some Lordship or other. Inevitably, the size of many commons was reduced. Between 1086 when the Domesday Book was completed and 1348, the date of the Black Death, the population of England and Wales had increased from about one and half million to almost four million. The increased population needed more resources and led to a demand to produce more food. Woods were being cleared and made into arable fields; marshes were drained for pasture and land was cultivated higher up the hillsides. There was increasing pressure on the use of common land. Less land and more animals meant that unrestricted pasturing had to be controlled and some regulation had to be enforced to limit the number of animals pastured on the common and on the fields after harvest. This was known as 'stinting'. The allocation was still generous by later standards as can be seen by the rights on a common in Leicestershire in 1256. For every yardland (about 30 acres) of arable land that a man held in the open fields he was permitted to pasture 2 horses, 4 oxen and cows, 30 sheep, 4 pigs and 5 geese, with all their offspring. This must have put considerable pressure on the common and wastes of the village.

The Lords of the Manor could see rich pickings in the large areas of waste and common in their domain, and used common land to create new farms and, in some cases, new towns. A good example of one of these towns is that of Liverpool which grew up on the common land alongside the river Mersey. First recorded in 1194, initially it had only seven streets one of which was called Moor Street.

Fencing around commons and turning them into fields greatly increased their value, but this interference created an imbalance in farming between arable and pasture and helped to fester tension between the village population and the Lord of the Manor. Records of the 13th and early 14th centuries contain details of many quarrels between the lords of the manor and peasantry over their respective rights over the common pastures. Peasants were accused of felling trees in woods they claimed to be common land. They also destroyed fences around woods and private parks and separate pastures which had been appropriated for private use.

The Statute of Merton, passed in 1236, was the first state intervention in the problem of common land. This statute authorised Manorial lords to enclose portions of the commons and wastes provided that sufficient pasture remained for their tenants.

Following the Black Death in 1345 the heavy mortality rate meant that there were not enough people to farm all the land and much of it was left uncultivated. The areas of commons and wastes once again expanded.

The social structure of a Manor such as Garway in the early middle ages would have contained various classes of people. Freeholders were a class whose property was not subject to the customs of the manor or to the will of the lord and could be disposed of without restriction. Customary or copyhold tenants were originally dependent upon the custom and the will of the lord, with obligations to perform certain services. The term copyhold arises from the title of the property being written in the Manor Court rolls and the tenant being given a 'copy'. When transferring the property this copy was surrendered to the lord who then gave it to the next tenant on the payment of a fine. Copyhold tenure was not abolished until 1922. However, after the Black Death and during the scarcity of labour that followed, many of the feudal services were commutated to money payments.

A large proportion of the population would be classed as villeins. This was a general term in use after the Norman Conquest to describe an unfree tenant who held his land subject to agricultural services and fines. His daughter could not marry without the lord's permission and on his death, a heriot (fine) was paid by his heirs. Once again, the Black Death was the cause of a change in the social structure as, because of the shortage of labour, the villein gained a better bargaining position and his tenure gradually became copyhold.

One of the lowest ranks in feudal society was the bordar or cottar. He had some land which barely provided subsistence for his family, but was obliged to work for the lord doing both agricultural and menial tasks either free or for a fixed sum.

The commons and wastes were an essential part of the day-to-day living for the country people right up to the early 19th century. There was no nipping to the shops for something forgotten; use was made of all the resources of the neighbourhood and nothing was wasted. The manorial tenants had rights to take timber from the common for their use. This was known as bote and came in various forms:

Cartbote – the right to take wood from the common to make or repair carts.

Firebor or Ferbote – the right to take wood from the common for fuel.

Foldbote – the right to take wood from the common to make sheep folds.

Haybote or Heybote or Hedgebote – the right to take wood from the common to make or repair fences.

Housebote – the right to take wood from the common to build or repair houses.

Ploughbote – the right to take wood from the common to make or repair ploughs.

The right of bote was one of the most important rights to the medieval villager. Think of all the building materials and fuel we have recourse to in the 21st century. Until the industrial revolution all of these needs would have been be met by the use of wood. Timber was used for the building of houses, the building of ships and for making tools of all kinds. It was the most widely used form of fuel. Vast quantities would have been converted to charcoal for iron making.

The grazing of animals played a major part in the agricultural economy of the parish. In an age which was devoid of supplementary cattle food such as turnips, kale and cattle cake, it was important that animals had access to pasture land. The farmer's wife also made good use of the common land for the collecting of berries, herbs and many wild plants used to make cordials, preserves, medicines and dyes. Teazles, besom brooms, brushwood harrows, pegs and baskets would be made from the growth of underwood and various bushes.

By the end of the 16th century the population of England and Wales had once again risen and most commons were subject to stinting. From the 16th to 18th centuries, parliamentary Enclosure Acts caused a number of commons to disappear and many to be reduced in size. Some of this was through agreement between the Lord and his copyhold tenants, but much was high-handed action that was often resisted.

Common land was also reduced due to the encroachment by the rural poor who erected small cottages and enclosed gardens. These buildings (many of which are still there today, usually updated and extended and now often very expensive) are dotted around many areas of common land in a haphazard fashion and often form islands in the middle of it. It was believed that if a cottager could erect his cottage, or rather hovel, in one night on the common, with smoke coming from his chimney before sunrise, he had established his right as a squatter on the waste. This he did at his own expense and mostly with his own hands. To this he would add a garth or garden on which he and his family would work hard to make it productive. In Wales such places were known as *ty-un-nos,* (the house of one night).

These settlements at the edges of the common land were where the craftsmen/traders were frequently to be found. In the 19th century particularly, smiths, shoemakers, tailors, coopers and small shopkeepers set up their businesses, a good example being Charlie Ruck's grandfather, Timothy Baldwin who had a business at the forge, Garway common.

Garway Hill Common

In 1805, John Duncumb wrote his *General View of the Agriculture of the County of Hereford*, in which he noted:

> The cottages in Herefordshire are generally of very humble and inferior construction: many are built on waste ground by their proprietor, whose means are far from adequate to the attainment of comfort and convenience.

He went on to praise some cottages that had been built at Holmer 'for the accommodation of poor families, not requiring more extensive apartments'. These cottages were built for £32 10s, and contained on the ground floor one room in front, twelve feet by fourteen, and six feet and a half high; also a small room behind. Above was a bedchamber of the same size as the front room below. There was a small garden for each cottage. How many people must have been crammed into these tiny living spaces, with no water and no sanitation and little regard to their health or well-being?

Between the 14th and the 17th centuries the face of the countryside gradually changed, as did farming practice. From 1800 there was a widespread campaign for a more effective use of land resources with particular reference to the remaining open fields and to the vast areas of common lands and wastes. In the open field system, where it existed, the strips were amalgamated, the furlongs divided and a patchwork of fields enclosed by hedges gradually developed. There is no evidence that the open field system was ever used in Garway — the hilly nature of the district may have been unsuitable for such a system of agriculture.

In compensation for loosing his strip in the common field a man may have been allotted no more than an acre, with perhaps a small cash payment for the loss of his rights in the common waste where he had been in the habit of grazing a cow that supplied his children with milk. He probably could not afford to erect fences around his solitary acre and, in any case, it would not have supported his cow. He therefore had to sell both his cow and his land. If the small farmer did take up his small allotment he may live to regret doing so. He would have still required horses or possibly oxen to plough his land but would not have the benefit of turning them on the common pasture to graze.

Many of the common lands were overstocked and in poor condition. In 1794 a reporter for the newly founded Board of Agriculture wrote the following report on the state of the commons in Shropshire:

> ... the idea of leaving them in their unimproved state to bear chiefly gorse bushes and fern is now completely scouted except by a few who have falsely conceived that the enclosing of them is an injury to the poor; but if these persons had seen as much of the contrary effects in that respect as I have I am fully persuaded their opposition would at once cease. Let those who doubt go round the commons now open, and view the miserable huts and poor, ill-cultivated, impoverished spots erected or rather thrown together and inclosed by themselves for which they pay 6d. or 1s. a year; which by loss of time both to the man and his family affords them a very trifle towards their maintenance, yet operates on their minds as a sort of independence; this idea leads the man to lose many a day's work by which he gets into a habit of indolence; a daughter kept at home to mind a half-starved cow, who being open to temptations soon turns harlot, and becomes a distrest [*sic*] ignorant mother instead of making a good house servant. The surrounding farmers, by this means, have neither industrious labourers or servants, for most certain it is that in the counties where this is the case the labourers are generally indolent, and the contrary is the case where they live under the farmer in comfortable cottages, work every day in the year with only a quarter of an acre of land, and have their children taught to read and put out to labour early.

William Marshall, another great agricultural writer at this time, said that 'common pastures and common fields are in their original intention and ever have been in their use, inseparable as animal life and food'. Most of the criticism referred to lowland commons, as the upland commons were generally well managed and vital to the type of farming practised in these areas.

Enclosure

Ever since the Middle Ages open fields, commons and wastes had gradually been enclosed for agricultural purposes. The open field strips were enclosed into small, hedged fields for better individual tillage. As farming practice improved and the population grew, farms needed large, consolidated tracts of land so that the new machinery and crop rotation could work efficiently. The enclosure of common land was deeply resented and resulted in riot and rebellion.

However, enclosure was fairly small scale until the 18th century. The earliest known private Enclosure Act awarded in 1607 related to some parishes in Herefordshire. Between 1760 and 1797 there were some 1,500 such Acts passed by Parliament which divided up common land, redistributed plots and required farmers to build fences around their land. As a result large landowners generally gained more land and although, in theory, the poor were compensated for the loss of common rights, they were often unable to get a living out of the small plots that they were allocated.

The General Enclosure Act of 1801 obviated the need for private Enclosure Acts that were both costly and time-consuming. In 1836 legislation was passed authorizing enclosures if two-thirds of the interested parties agreed and in 1854 the Enclosures Commission was established. The Commissioners reported to Parliament and were authorised to allocate common land for 'exercise' and 'recreation'. These Commissioners travelled round to the different villages to supervise the enclosure of the land. Between 1750 and 1850 there were approximately 4,000 Enclosure Acts of Parliament and 7 million acres of land were fenced.

The process of obtaining an Act of Parliament started when the owners of at least three-quarters of the land in a parish decided that they wished to enclose. They then produced a petition giving notice to the rest of the parish. This petition had to be fixed to the church door for three consecutive Sundays in late August or early September and maybe also in the local newspaper. The Bill of Enclosure was drafted for the parish and read twice in the House of Commons. After studying the Bill, a Parliamentary Committee considered objections and wrote any alterations. The third reading in the House of Commons was followed by that in the House of Lords and if passed, given the Royal Assent and so became an Act of Parliament. Every farmer who received an allocation of land had to pay a share of the cost of the proceedings. Once again it was the small farmer with little capital who was unduly burdened.

When it was decided to enclose land in a parish, the commissioners (between three and twelve depending on the amount of land to be enclosed) were appointed. They would appoint surveyors to draw up a plan of the village with its fields and strips, along with the names of the owners of this land, which were recorded on the map. At a series of meetings the landowners would claim the land they wanted awarded under the enclosure and the commissioners would decided who would actually receive land in the award. When all the land had been allocated a new map was produced displaying the new enclosures, boundaries between each section, and the location of new paths and roads.

The effect upon the rural poor was to drive many of them into the towns where the Industrial Revolution was gaining momentum. For those who remained, the larger farms needed more labour; more stockmen, shepherds and ploughmen.

Up to the beginning of the 19th century the common land on Garway Hill stretched all the way to Orcop Hill. In addition to the 209 acres of Garway Hill common there were 275 acres of common land in the parish of Orcop. The Enclosure Award for Orcop was granted between 1814 and 1824, when common land was divided up into 125 parcels of land, most plots being less than five acres and several plots less than ten perches, just enough to build a small cottage with a garden. Mr Thomas Hampton Symons, the Lord of the Manor of Orcop, who lived at The Mynde, Much Dewchurch, was awarded 17 plots of land amounting to about 60 acres which he then sub-let to various tenants.

Although there had been some encroachment on Orcop common over the years it was the Enclosure Award that precipitated the building of many small houses with their accompanying plots of land. Many of the buildings scattered around Garway Hill can be dated to this event.

3   Lords of the Manor of Garway

Garway Hill common and all of the other areas of common land in Garway have always been part of the Manor of Garway and as such have belonged to the Lord of the Manor. However, there has never been a 'big house' in Garway, home to the Lord of the Manor. In fact it is safe to say that few, if any, of the Lords of the Manor ever visited Garway but it is interesting to know who they were and how their influence has shaped the parish as it is today. The Manor of Garway and the parish of Garway have the same boundaries except for a small area where the Manor extended into the parish of Kentchurch (see Custumal, overleaf). Stewards were appointed to administer the Manor on their behalf and these stewards in their turn appointed the local officials. The steward presided at the Manor Courts which were known as the Court Baron and the Court Leet where a jury of local men enforced the Customs of the Manor. The main business consisted of surrenders of land, dower administrations and the use of common fields and wastes. These courts appointed a reeve who was responsible for collecting the dues, a hayward to look after the commons and sometimes a woodward. The tenants were expected to attend and anyone who was absent without reasonable excuse was fined. The Court Baron was held at Broad Oak, once a fortnight, on Thursdays. The Court Leet was usually held only once or twice a year within one month after Easter Day and within one month after the Feast of St Michaels. One of the customs of this Court stated that all tenants, whether free or customary living within the Manor, had free rights of pasture and pannage in and over the commons and waste grounds, namely Garway Hill, Pengarstone Gorst and the Little Common called The Moor alias the Heald and other waste ground within the Manor. This custom was reconfirmed at a Court held in 1827. The Court Leet dealt with petty offences such as common nuisances, highway or ditch repairs and encroachment on the common lands. At this Court they elected the constable, aletaster, pinder (pound keeper) and any other minor officials to enforce the by-laws. Every male over the age of 12 was obliged to attend. All the transactions of these Courts were written down on the Court Rolls, so-called as these were pieces of paper which were rolled up. Most of them have since been lost. Starting in 1799 and ending in 1945, the records for the Garway Manor were written in books and these books, which are preserved in Hereford County Record Office, are available to be read. They are hand written and contain some very interesting hand drawn and coloured maps.

The Manorial system developed following the Norman Conquest and the records of the Manor of Garway go back to the date when Henry II gave land to the Knights Templar.

The grant was confirmed on 16 July 1199 when King John transferred to the Templars 2,000 acres of land in Garway. The Templars built their traditional round church with monastic buildings and farmed the land to provide revenue to support the fighting in the Holy Land during the Crusades. Very soon after the suppression of the Templars in 1307, the Manor was given to their rival Order the Knights Hospitaller and so it became part of their Manor of Dinmore. After administering the Manor for over 200 years, until the time of the Reformation in 1538, the Knights Hospitaller were dissolved and their property, including the Manor of Garway, became crown property.

The Manor of East Greenwich was the name of a Royal Manor in East Kent that held crown property and also manors that had been confiscated by Henry VIII. The tenure of land held from the crown 'as of the Manor of East Greenwich' soon became a recognised

---

10th Article of Custom

To the 10th Article we the Jury do find present and declare to the utmost of our memory and knowledge which the memory of man is not to the contrary that – the ancient and general Boundary or Boundaries of this manor of Garway aforesaid do extend.
Beginning at a place called the Darren and thence along a certain way to certain lands called March Hill, thence from the farther part of that lands down to the river Monnow and along the said river Monnow to a small parcel of land called the Kemp Pleck and over the said river and around about the same into the said river and thence along the said river to another parcel of land called the King's Pleck and round about the same into the said river and thence along the said river to a place called Cawros Rocks and over the said river and around about a parcel of meadow formerly the lands of John Hayles and now of John Scudamore Esq Gent, and thence along the upper side of a little meadow called the Grove meadow and thence by ancient marks and mears dividing the Parish of Kentchurch and the parish of Garway to Lanhithogg and thence along a way to the house of Ruben Meredith and along a little brook and mears to Bagarlidiatt and thence along a way and hedge and ditch to a mear stone upon the Hill and thence along an old ditch from mear stone to mear stone to a place called the Guard and thence to an old House Gate now in the tenure of Richard Rogers and thence along a way to a House formerly Cathring Turnor now Walter Meredith, and thence through the land of Chandos Lloyd Gent to Trollways Brook and thence through and between by marks the lands of Richard Price and Chandos Lloyd aforesaid into the Way leading from Pengarstone to Treagoe and thence by certain known mears and marks to Broad Oaks and thence through the Mansion House called Calldicote and thence to a mear stone in the brook called Nant-y-waine and thence to Black Wood and thence to the Way leading from Broad Oak towards Monmouth and from the said way by mears to Hazelfield and thence along an Old Ditch through the lands formerly of Wm Vaughan Gent deceased and now the lands of Henry Milbourne Esq to the Darren aforesaid.

The Custumal of 1678 A Description of the Boundary of the Manor of Garway
(F35 RC/HT/1-7 Hereford County Record Office)

formula for the granting or selling of manors and had the advantage that it confirmed on the inhabitants of the manor all of their ancient laws and privileges.

James I granted the Manor of Garway out of the Manor of East Greenwich in 1611. I have not seen the Patent Roll and do not know to whom it was granted. However, sometime between 1611 and 1649, the Manor of Garway was held by William Garway or Garraway, a merchant of the City of London. There is no way of knowing whether or not he had any connection with Garway or whether his name was just a coincidence.

In 1649 William Garway sold the Manor of Garway to Thomas Pearle, a silk merchant from the parish of Allhallows in the City of London. Pearle appointed Charles Milbourne of Llanrothal as his steward and after Charles' death in 1662 his son, Henry Milbourne, a member of the Middle Temple in London, succeeded him as steward for which he received 20% of the income of the Manor.

By 1691 the Manor of Garway had again been sold, this time to Sir William Compton who lived at Hindlip House in Worcestershire. For many generations Hindlip had been the home of the Habington family and passed down in this line until 1686 when Thomas Habington died childless and left the property to his cousin Sir William Compton. It was about the time when he succeeded to the estate at Hindlip that Sir William Compton bought the Manor of Garway. For the next 150 years the Manor of Garway descended through the female line and was not sold again until 1919.

The story of Sir William Compton and his family reads like an historical romance, complete with villain and is told in a letter written by Robert Berkley in 1805 when he was 87 years of age. (Ref D641. Staffordshire Record Office).

Sometime early in the 18th century Sir William Compton married his dairymaid. They had four children, William, Walter, Catherine and Jane. Sir William died in 1758 and in his will appointed Robert Berkley of Spetchley in Worcestershire as a Trustee. The eldest son, now Sir William, inherited the estate but no provision had been made for his mother, brother or sisters, and Lady Compton contested the will with the help of Mr Berkley. William engaged Mr Bearcroft, a solicitor, to look after his affairs but before he reached the age of 21 he died, leaving a young widow. This is when things really began to get complicated. The residue of William's personal estate was left to his widow and the Compton Estate, including the Manor of Garway passed to his brother, Walter (now Sir Walter) and to his sisters Catherine and Jane.

Mr Bearcroft turned out to be the villain. He prevailed upon Catherine Compton to run away with him to Scotland were they were married thus acquiring her portion of the estate. He did not get away with this as he was sent to the Fleet prison in London for marrying a Ward of the Court of Chancery. Following his eventual release he returned to Worcestershire and started spreading malicious gossip about old Lady Compton and her friends whereby she again appealed to Robert Berkley for help.

Meanwhile, Sir Walter had got into bad company and took off to Scotland to marry a Miss Mosley. On their return they settled in a house in Herefordshire, but before long they had separated and he returned to Hindlip where he was seized with 'a violent disorder'. Mr Bearcroft and his wife Catherine took Sir Walter to their house at Hartbury in

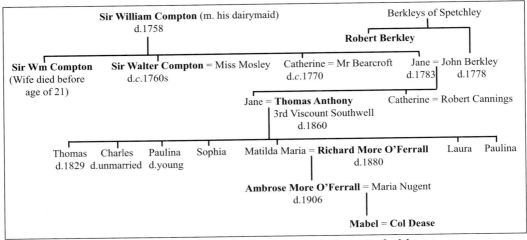

A family tree showing the Lords of the Manor in bold type

Gloucestershire where they tried to persuade him to disinherit his younger sister, Jane, and give all of his estates to his older sister, Catherine Bearcroft. Once again Lady Compton appealed to Robert Berkely for help and they decided to appoint another solicitor, Mr Welsh of Evesham, to file a bill to prevent this happening. Some time later Sir Walter died and his executors gave Robert Berkley the authority to revive the bill against Mr Bearcroft.

Sir Walter had often expressed his gratitude to Robert Berkley for all he had done for the family and suggested that maybe his sister Jane might marry Robert's younger brother, John Berkley. Soon after Walter's death this wedding took place.

Numerous lawsuits and contests ensued but Catherine Bearcroft was protected as she had by this time separated from her husband. In order to prevent her being forced to settle the whole estate on Mr Bearcroft, Mr Thurlow, the then Attorney General advised that Mrs Bearcroft execute a deed in pursuance of her power of appointment and settle in moieties (usually a half portion of an estate) on herself and her sister, which put an end to some of the contests. Catherine died at Hartpury about a year later, but even so, the Chancery suits carried on for many years.

John Berkley died in 1778 leaving his widow, Jane, and two young daughters also called Catherine and Jane. Their affairs were still in an awful mess and Robert was persuaded to take over the management of the estates (which included the Manor of Garway). The lawsuits continued for many years and after Jane died in about the year 1783, Robert became Guardian and Trustee of the infants Catherine and Jane Berkley. They were described as two very sickly children, and Robert Berkley and his wife cared for them for more than 20 years until their marriage. He therefore, during this period of Guardianship became Lord of the Manor of Garway.

The Compton family were Roman Catholics. In the early 18th century the law required Roman Catholic landowners to register all of their real estate and in 1715 Sir William Compton filed a return for his land within the County of Hereford. For Garway he lists

All that capital messuage tenement and farm called Cwmaddock now in his own possession and all that messuage tenement and lands and farm called the Old Garden now in the possession of John Meredith at a yearly rent of £17 all which premises are lying within the Parish of Garway in the said County of Hereford.

The document goes on to mention farms called Longmores, Lodge Farm, Church Farm, Colesman's Farm and also several cottages whose rents range between 1s 6d and 6s 8d a year. Also mentioned are the tithes, the mill and the coppice woods.

As would be expected, Jane Berkley married a Roman Catholic and following her marriage the Manor of Garway became the jointly owned property of Jane and her husband, Thomas Anthony, Viscount Southwell (pronounced 'Suthell') who was an Irish Peer. By 1810, Thomas Wakeman of the Graig, Cross Ash had been appointed steward of the Manor. He was a solicitor, a staunch Roman Catholic and an eminent local historian.

Lord Southwell rarely, if ever came to Garway. In a letter to John Scudamore at Kentchurch Court written in November 1835 on the subject of the new road proposed at Demesne pitch, he says '… it would seem to benefit our tenants in Garway, but from my ignorance of the locality …'. In the same letter he declines an invitation from John Scudamore to shoot pheasants as he is leaving to spend the winter on the south coast, or even France, on account of his youngest daughter's very delicate state of health.

Lord and Lady Southwell had a large family, consisting of two sons and five daughters. The third daughter, Matilda-Maria, was to inherit the Garway estate. She was married in September 1839 to the Right Hon Richard More O'Ferrall who was Member of Parliament for Kildare from 1830-1846 and from 1859-1865. Lord Melbourne appointed him Lord of the Treasury and in 1839 Secretary to the Admiralty. During the years 1847-51 he was Governor of Malta. Richard died aged 83 on 27 October 1880 at Kingtown near Dublin. Their son and heir was Ambrose More O'Ferrall of Balyna House, Kildare who in 1860 married Maria Anne, daughter of Sir William Nugent.

Ambrose and Maria were the first Lord and Lady of the Manor to visit

Notice of a Court Leet and Court Baron to be held under Ambrose More O'Ferrall

and take a personal interest in Garway. In 1875 they built Glanmonnow House on land that had been part of New House Farm. On Ambrose's death in 1906, his daughter Mabel inherited the Garway Estate and the Lordship of the Manor. She lived in Tipperary, Ireland and was married to Major Dease, the local magistrate. Glanmonnow House was rented to a Captain Walford at a rent of £285 per annum that was replaced in 1916 by a yearly tenancy at a War Rent of £150 per annum. In 1919 Mrs Mabel Dease offered the Garway Estate for sale.

Arthur Ernest Lawley, a Manchester businessman whose family had made their money in shipping and cotton, had recently bought Hilston Park at Skenfrith. At the end of 1919 Arthur Lawley contracted to buy the Garway Estate. He clearly intended keeping only part of it because he instructed John D. Wood & Company of Mount Street, London to put the majority of the estate up for sale on 14 January 1920.

The Garway Estate, sold in 61 lots, comprised of 2751 acres that included Glanmonnow House, 15 stock and mixed farms, 20 smallholdings and cottages with grazing rights on Garway commons. The total area of the parish of Garway at that time was 3.614 acres. Not included in the sale was the Lordship of the Manor or the fishing rights on the river Monnow which were retained by Mr Lawley.

On Saturday 17 January 1920 there was a report in the *Hereford Times* of the results of the sale the previous Wednesday. Neither Glanmonnow House nor New House Farm was sold. Neither were Cwm Maddoc Farm (330 acres), Garway Court (187 acres), Great Demesne Farm (297 acres), Darren Mill and cottage, Lower Newland and about ten other lots. Most of the tenants had been given the opportunity to purchase their holdings privately and many of them had done so, presumably before the auction sale.

Garden fête at Glanmonnow in 1907

Arthur Ernest Lawley died on 26 May 1920 aged 45. The report in the *Monmouth Beacon* two days later announced 'the death of Mr Lawley of Hilston Park, near Monmouth which took place on Wednesday morning after a brief illness. The deceased was a keen angler. In fact it was only on Thursday of last week that he caught a chill while fishing and this set up the illness which resulted fatally, despite the best of medical attention. He leaves a widow and two daughters.'

Arthur Lawley had bought the Garway Estate for £37,550, a transaction that was completed just a few days before his sudden death. Just two days before he died there was recorded in the Manor Court Rolls for Garway that a Court Baron was held, the heading of which is as follows:

> Manor of Garway in the County of Hereford. Before John Trewren Vizard of the town of Monmouth, Gentleman, Deputy Steward of Arthur Ernest Lawley Esquire, Lord of the said Manor on the Twenty-fourth of May One Thousand Nine Hundred and Twenty.

Mrs Elizabeth Wright Lawley and her two young daughters, Christine (known as Kitty) and Joyce, were now left with the huge Hilston Park House and Estate at Skenfrith and all the unsold portions of the Garway Estate including Glanmonnow House. To complicate matters, Mr Lawley's will could not be found and Mrs Lawley dealt with the Garway Estate as Administratrix of her husband's estate and in this capacity she became Lady of the Manor of Garway. (The will was in fact found later in the year and gave his father as one of the executors.)

The Hilston Park Estate with 3,371 acres of land was offered for auction in May 1921. This sale included Glanmonnow House which had been renamed the Dower House and was for sale with 1,130 acres of land and fishing rights on the river Monnow. The purchaser was The Newcombe Estates Company Limited of Market Harborough, Leicestershire. They paid £53,500 for the whole estate, including the property in Garway. On 4 November 1921 John D. Wood and Company held another sale at the Beaufort Arms, Monmouth this time of Glanmonnow House, including the home farm (New House Farm) and all the unsold parts of the Hilston Park Estate. Mrs Lawley and her daughters left Hilston Park in February 1922 and moved to Harewood House, Hanover Square, London and eventually to Old Place, Aldwick, Bognor Regis.

Mrs Elizabeth Lawley, lady of the manor of Garway, with her daughter, Joyce, at their home, Old Place, Bognor Regis, in 1943 (Sir Peter de la Billière)

Kelly's *Directories* for Herefordshire in the editions for 1926, 1934 and 1941 refer to Mrs Lawley as the Lady of the Manor. Messrs Boote, Edgar & Company of 53 Spring Gardens, Manchester, the solicitors who had acted for her husband, were still acting for Mrs Lawley in 1944. This legal practice is in fact still operating in Manchester at the present time.

When the registration of the common lands throughout Britain took place in the late 1960s an effort was made to try and find Mrs Lawley or her descendents. For whatever reason this was unsuccessful and so Garway Parish Council registered all of the common land in the parish so that it would not be lost. Mrs Lawley died in fact at Bognor Regis, where she had lived for many years, on 30 October 1968 and according to the 'latest wills' column in *The Times* for December 1968 she left £96,936. It should have been quite easy to trace her descendants from the probate records of that time. Failure to do so resulted in much confusion over the ownership of the common land and was to result in a most unfortunate misunderstanding. In 2003, Garway Parish Council, believing that they owned the common, encouraged the Parish Hall Trustees to obtain planning permission to build a large community hall and car park on Garway Common close to the playing field. The parish was split between those who wanted the hall on the common and those who were against any building on common land. The majority of the commoners were against this building.

An application known as a 'Section 194' was made to the Secretary of State as required by law. The whole question was considered by DEFRA who decided that the best way to unravel this confusion was to hold a Public Inquiry. This in due course took place over a period of three days in April 2007. Mr Trevor Cookson, a high ranking planning inspector, headed the Inquiry that was held in Garway Parish Hall and which gave both supporters and objectors of the scheme ample opportunity to express their wishes and opinions. In June 2007, Mr Cookson, in a lengthy and detailed document, announced that the Secretary of State had ruled against this application to build on common land thus bringing to a close an unfortunate and divisive state of affairs.

Although Mrs Lawley never came back to Garway she had remained in touch for many years through her agent. Before leaving Hilston Park she conveyed the Parish Room to the Parish Council and there is a note in the Parish Council Minutes for 22 March 1922, thanking Mrs Lawley for the gift of the site. In the Manor Court Rolls which continued until 1944, the remaining copyholds on property in Garway were extinguished under the signature of Mrs Lawley.

Joyce Lawley never married and remained living with her mother. Elizabeth Christine Lawley, the younger daughter, was married in 1933 to an officer in the Royal Navy, Surgeon Lieutenant Commander Denis de Labilliere. He was the son of the Vicar of Llangattock who had conducted the memorial service at St Maughan's church for Arthur Lawley in 1920. In April 1934, their first son, Peter, was born followed in August 1937 by Michael. At the outbreak of the Second World War, Commander de Labilliere was serving on the cruiser HMS *Fiji* when in May 1941 the ship was sunk by German bombers off the coast of Crete and he was reported missing, presumed drowned. Kitty was remarried in 1943 to Major Maurice Bennetts who was then serving in the RAF Regiment and her third son, David Bennetts, was born in July 1944.

Elizabeth Lawley died on 30 August 1968 at the Nyecroft Nursing Home, Bognor Regis. During her last years she had been blind and bedridden although still very mentally alert. In her will written in 1962 she left the residue of her estate in trust to her three grandsons. This of course, included the Lordship of the Manor of Garway, although none of the three young men, very busy with their careers, realized the significance of this title. One of the Trustees of Mrs Lawley's will was James Herbert Ogden of Manchester who, surprisingly, in 2007 is still alive and acting on behalf of the estate.

The Lordship of the Manor of Garway is now held jointly between General Sir Peter de la Billière, his half-brother, David Bennetts, and the sons of the late Michael de Labilliere. (It is interesting to note the subtle change of spelling to the family surname).

The role of Lord of the Manor is now almost exclusively involved with common land. Unfortunately, many Lordships have been brought into disrepute by being bought up by unscrupulous profiteers who exploit their ownership by fleecing the owners of the properties around their common land by charging them for vehicular access. The de la Billière family place great value in the preservation of all of the common land in Garway and they will do all they can to conserve this valuable asset for the use and enjoyment of future generations.

*General Sir Peter de la Billière (top)
and Mr David Bennetts (lower), Lords of the
Manor of Garway (Sir Peter de la Billière)*

Extracts from The Manor Court Rolls of Garway

Court Baron held at Broad Oak 1799.
James Croft, Steward. Robert Berkley, Lord of the Manor.

In 1808 the Court Baron was held at the home of Mary Smith, of Broad Oak, widow.
The Right Honorable Thomas Anthony Viscount Southwell of the Kingdom of Ireland and Robert Cannings Esq are Lords of the said Manor.

1809.1809.1809James Croft, Steward

30.4.1810
Thomas Wakeman, Steward.
Lands of the said John Matthews and the Common called Garway Hill and the lands heretofore of Thomas Williams now of the Roman Catholic Clergy.

10.10.1810
Following persons are presented for encroachment on the wastes and severally fined twenty shillings each unless the same be laid open before 25th March next.

5/- Walter Williams on Garway Gorst
2/6 John Meredith by Coedyago turnpike
2/6 James Preece Garway Gorst
2/6 Thomas Gwatkin Lower Common
2/6 James Pritchard by the Three Brookes
2/6 Edward Parry Lower Common
2/6 Thomas Morgan
5/- Paul Meredith Garway Hill
2/6 John Evans Cawros Rocks
2/6 Thomas Weaver Lower Common
2/6 James Phillips   "
5/- James Cotton   "
2/6 Thomas Gwatkin   "
2/6 Richard Williams Garway Hill
2/6 James Gritton   "
2/6 John Harris   "
2/6 Edward Castrey   "
2/6 Edward Maddox   Garway Gorst
5/- John Bradford   Lower Common

Continued encroachment – they are amerced – fined.

5.10.1816

Present an encroachment on Garway Hill by Edward Castry (6d), John Powell (6d) and on the roadside near Garway common by Francis Price. Also two encroachments on Garway common by Edward Maddox (1/-) and Thomas Saunders (1/6), all since the last court.

We present that a path through the fields belonging to the Lodge Farm within the jurisdiction of the court is obstructed and very dangerous by the opening of a quarry by Thomas Herbert tenant to the Lord of the Manor, and that the same is a common nuisance and to be fenced out immediately.

It is presented by the Court that all persons herein above presented for encroachments or continuing the same do lay the same open before the next Court under pain each one of two guineas. Thomas Edwards appointed Petty Constable.

17.10.1817

William Vaughan, Bailiff.
Thomas Edwards, Petty constable reappointed.
John Powell, Garway Hill, Hayward.

Presentment. All those who were presented at the last court for encroachment upon the waste lands of the Lord of the said Manor and that have not thrown the same open, incurred the fine of 2 guineas.

With the consent of the Homage the following persons agreed to rent the encroachment by them made as below at the rents below as tenants from year to year from Ladyday 1816:

Thomas Taylor. An encroachment on Pengarstone Gorst and a cottage by himself built thereon adjoining the Turnpike Road. 0. 2s. 6d.
Paul Meredith. An encroachment on Garway Hill 0. 2s. 6d.
Thomas Saunders An encroachment on Pengarstone Gorst in front of his house at Caer (Duff) and adjoining thereto. 0. 1s. 0d.

Presentment that the highway leading from Garway Cross towards Little Garway is very dangerous and impassable and ought to be repaired by the Parish of Garway.

Presentment. Thomas Bradford and Sophia Bradford his sister for breaking open the manor pound in the night time and taking out a pig belonging to their father which had been impounded therein.

28.5.1824 (From the Scudamore Papers)

John Lucy Scudamore's right to turn on the common on Garway Hill. If the recipient denies the right, please inform Lord Southwell and his agent that the writer is determined to try that right, and will order Mr Scudamore's attorney, Mr Cleave to commence an action against the recipient if sheep marked JLS are not released tonight.

10.5.1827

ITEM   Leet and View of Frankinpledge ought to be held within the said Manor twice a year (viz) within one month after Easterday and within one month after the Feast of St Michaels yearly but that the said Courts have been for many years past held only once a year. And also that the Court Baron ought to be held within the said Manor once a fortnight upon Thursdays, for the recovery of small debts under forty shillings, and the dispatch of such other business as belongs to the said Court; But Courts of Baron or Customary Courts for the surrender and admission to Estates may be held on any day of the week at the Lord's pleasure.

ITEM That at the Court Leet time out of mind a Constable had been chosen for the Parish of Garway within the said Manor.

ITEM That the freehold tenants of the said Manor hold their several lands and tenements in Free Soccage, tenure by frailty, suit of court, and the several rates as expressed in the Rolls. And that on the death of every free tenant of the said Manor, there is due to the Lord a relief which reliefs are certain and fixed but the amount the said Jurors know not. But two years of chief rent has usually been taken for many years past.

ITEM All tenants, whether free or customary inhabiting within the Manor, have free common of pasture and pannage in and over the commons and waste grounds there viz Garway Hill, Pengarstone Gorst and the Little Common called The Moor alias the Heald and other waste ground within the Manor.

27.4.1835

William Hooper, Steward   Viscount Southwell, Lord of the Manor.
William Lewis, Bailiff, Benjamin Price and James Maddox, Constables.
Davis Embry, Hayward, James Willett, Pound Keeper.

Present – John Powell, Mason of Garway Hill for having fallen an Ash Tree property of the Lord of the Manor on a Green Lane adjoining Garway Hill.
Present – William Read for turning water out of its former channel on Garway Hill to the great injury of the neighbours.

22.4.1851

Hayward rescued certain cattle from Garway Hill.
William Holleys seized for trespass on Garway Hill Common.

5.4.1852

Present Thomas Prosser and Thomas Watkins for cutting and hauling fern and gorst on Garway Hill.

10.4.1886

Several people from other parishes depasture cattle upon Garway Hill and gather fern to the detriment of the tenants of the Manor. Walter Prosser Morgan and David Ellie Haywards for Garway Hill.

1891

William Barrell, appointed Hayward on Garway Hill.

4 Archaeology

As part of the 'Garway Hill Common Through The Ages' project, a series of archaeological investigations were conducted by the members of the local community with support from staff of Herefordshire Archaeology, (Herefordshire Council's archaeological service). Investigations began with a two-day walkover survey of the common, during which any archaeological features surviving as earthworks were recorded using global positioning by satellite (GPS) equipment. The results of this survey provided a detailed record of the archaeological resource upon the common and greatly enhanced our understanding of how the use of the common has changed throughout its history. The results of the walkover were supported by aerial photography and the use of Light Detection and Ranging (LIDAR). This combination of techniques helped to accurately locate individual sites and provided detailed information concerning the extent of earthworks relating to previous land use.

The results of this initial survey led to the detailed investigation of three specific sites. These consisted of two earthwork enclosures and an area containing the earthwork remains of linear boundaries forming an ancient field system. Earthworks relating to the two enclosures and field system were recorded using an Electronic Distance Meter (EDM) and drawing board to produce a series of measured plans.

The largest of the two earthwork enclosures was then subject to geophysical investigation. The results of the geophysical survey and measured plan were then used to determine the location of three trial trenches in order to provide the maximum amount of information regarding the use, origins and subsequent development of the enclosure. The three trenches were excavated over a period of two weeks, during which members of the local community were instructed in modern excavation techniques including feature recognition, the recording of individual layers and deposits, and the production of scaled drawings.

The resulting information gained from this suite of archaeological techniques has provided a detailed understanding of fascinating and often complex changes in land-use which have taken place upon Garway Hill Common from prehistoric times to the present day.

Plate 1 Aerial Photograph looking south-west across Garway Hill Common.
(© C. Musson & Herefordshire Archaeology [06-CN-0301/08])

Topography and Geology

Garway Hill Common is located at the summit of a conical hill at a maximum height of 366m OD. (1204 feet). The hill is steepest on the north, west and south sides where the land falls to form the base of the Monnow Valley. To the east the hill falls more gradually, narrowing to form a saddle from where it continues down slope in the form of a narrow spur.

The underlying geology of Garway Hill Common consists of Old Red Sandstone of the Breconian formation.

Garway Hill Common lies within the Parish of Garway, the parish boundary between Garway and Orcop intermittently following the eastern edge of the common.

Early People on the Common

The earliest evidence for human activity within the Monnow Valley derives from a series of flint tools discovered on and around Garway Hill Common. One of the highest concentrations of flints was recorded on the common, around the area of Black Pool, where natural weathering at the pool edges, together with erosion by animals coming to drink, revealed an assemblage of flint artefacts dating to the Neolithic Period (*c*.4000–2000 BC). As flints do not occur naturally within Herefordshire, such finds indicate human activity. The actual concentration of flints suggesting that the production of flint tools took place on Garway Hill. These tools included scrapers and blades probably used for the

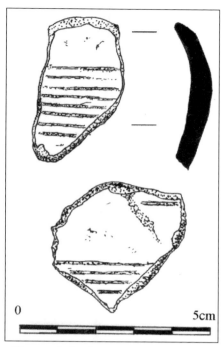

Figure 1 Early Bronze Age Beaker Pottery discovered at Little Garway Farm. (© Herefordshire Archaeology)

processing of animal carcasses, along with waste flakes, suggesting that a community was living in the vicinity and either using areas such as this for a seasonal hunting camp or perhaps a more permanent settlement, close to which they were rearing and slaughtering domestic animals.

Further evidence of early settlement in the area came from the south of the common at Little Garway Farm. Excavations during the Foot and Mouth Crisis of 2001 resulted in the discovery of a Bronze Age beaker burial. The fragmented remains of a beaker pot were retrieved when a stone lined cist burial was disturbed during the excavation of a disposal pit by a mechanical excavator.

Although these finds indicate activity on and in close proximity to Garway Hill Common during the Prehistoric period, there was, until the investigations of 'The Garway Hill Through The Ages' project, no confirmed evidence for actual settlement.

Then, as mentioned, two earthwork enclosures were recorded. One of these sites was only discovered through a series of aerial photographs taken as part of the project. The site is situated upon a natural terrace within the south-west of the common and

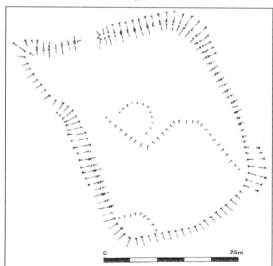

Figure 2 Scale plan of sub-rectangular enclosure. (© Herefordshire Archaeology)

Plate 2 Aerial photo of sub-rectangular enclosure. (© Herefordshire Archaeology & Chris Musson [06-CN-0218/20])

33

comprises a sub-rectangular enclosure (HSM 43902), approximately 40m long and 30m wide, with platforms within its centre. The ramparts of the enclosure consist of a simple bank with external ditch. The bank and ditch are very eroded and do not stand higher than 1m above the ground. The exact location of the entrance into the enclosure is unclear due to heavy bracken growth and the often subtle earthwork remains.

The second earthwork enclosure was looked at in greater detail. This was largely due to its accessibility and the fact that a number of suggestions had been made over the preceding years concerning its age and use. The enclosure (HSM 6251) is located close

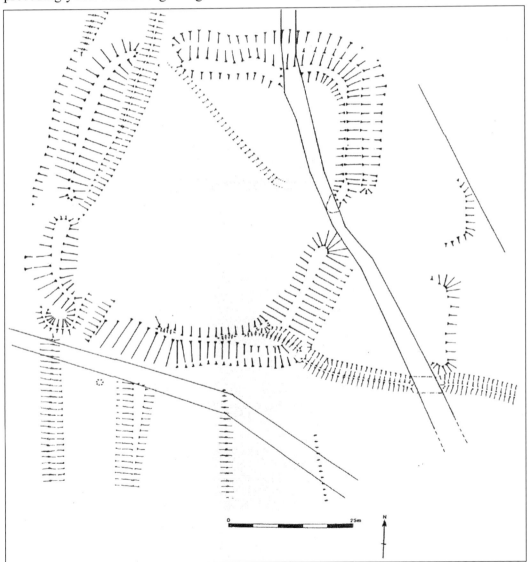

Figure 3 Scale Plan of rectangular enclosure within the south east of the common.
(© Herefordshire Archaeology)

to the south-east corner of the common, on a naturally formed terrace and has been the subject of speculation for many decades prior to 'The Garway Hill Through The Ages' project. The enclosure was added into the Sites and Monument Record in 1988 when it was interpreted as a Roman or possibly medieval industrial site. Besides some measured sketch plans produced in the late 1960s and early 1970s, no other fieldwork had been undertaken on the site. It measures approximately 90m in length and 70m wide, and is enclosed by a single bank and ditch. The bank survives to a maximum height of 2m and is up to 4m wide; the ditch is approximately 5m wide and survives to a depth of 1m. The entrance into the enclosure is on the eastern side where a pronounced break in the rampart approximately 3m wide can be seen.

The state of preservation of the ramparts varies considerably. Along the southern edge of the enclosure the ditch has been filled by the erosion of material used to construct the bank. Here the bank survives largely as a south-facing lynchet, or terrace, due to this

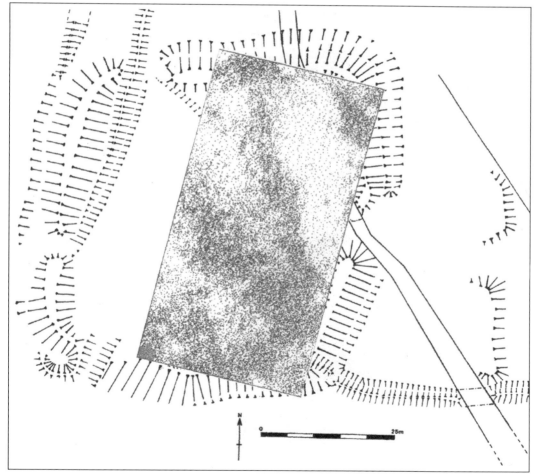

Figure 4 Geophysical Survey results within the settlement enclosure.
(© Herefordshire Archaeology)

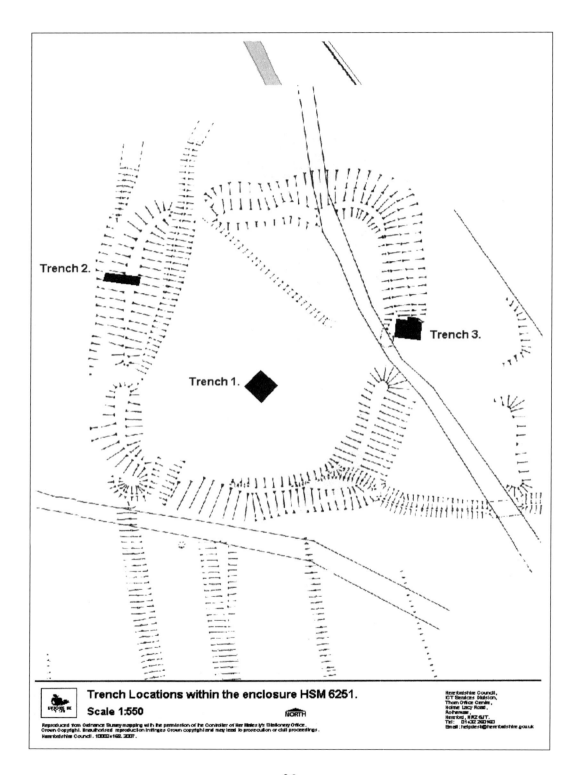

Trench 2.

Trench 3.

Trench 1.

Trench Locations within the enclosure HSM 6251.

Scale 1:550

NORTH

Herefordshire Council,
ICT Services Division,
Thorn Office Centre,
Holme Lacy Road,
Rotherwas,
Hereford, HR2 6JT.
Tel: 01432 260160
Email: helpdesk@herefordshire.gov.uk

collapse of material. Such erosion is likely to have occurred naturally, however at other locations on its circuit human interference has had a marked effect on the survival of the earthworks. The south-west corner of the enclosure has, for example, been removed by later quarrying, possibly during the post-medieval period.

Following the detailed measured survey of the large enclosure, members of the local community together with staff of Herefordshire Archaeology carried out a geophysical survey of the interior in order to determine the presence of any buried features that might indicate settlement. Two 30m² grids were positioned within the eastern half of the site next to the enclosure entrance. The survey instrument comprised a Geoscan RM 15 resistivity meter which records and compares levels of water resistance within the soil. Solid surfaces such as buried walls, roads, rubble and geology produce a high resistance reading, whereas buried ditches or pits retain more moisture than their surroundings and provide low resistance readings.

The results show a high level of high resistance within the enclosure, the scale of which may be caused by the underlying geology (indicated by the darker areas). However, the survey did pick up the inner edge of the rampart (bank) and the break where the entrance once was. The larger quantity of high readings within the southern portion of the grid suggested that this area may have been subjected to more disturbance, some of which may have been the result of human activity.

The investigations of the large enclosure continued into late June 2006. Based on the results of both the detailed measured survey and the geophysical survey, the locations of a series of small excavations were agreed. As a consequence three trenches were located and excavated with great enthusiasm and commitment by members of the local community and volunteers from surrounding parishes. Each trench was located with the aim to answer a number of questions regarding the enclosure's purpose and date.

Trench 1 was located within the interior of the enclosure toward the south-east corner where the geophysical results indicated the presence of possible human disturbance or buried structures. The siting of this trench was intended to record any evidence for occupation on the site.

Trench 2 was located to cut across the western rampart in order to recover information concerning the rampart's construction and subsequent abandonment.

Trench 3 was positioned over the ditch terminal immediately to the north of the presumed enclosure entrance. It was intended that this trench would confirm the presence of an entrance and hopefully provide an opportunity to recover dateable artefacts if none were forthcoming from *Trenches 1* and *2*. Ditch terminals are often found to contain large quantities of artefacts either through intentional deposition or slighting / ditch infilling.

The two-week excavation proved to be highly successful despite the limited size of the trenches, the largest, (*Trench 1*), being only 5m square. After many decades of postulation concerning the date of the enclosure, pottery recovered from *Trench 1* and particularly *Trench 3* indicated that the enclosure had been constructed and occupied during the middle to late Iron Age. The majority of the pottery was recovered from the fill of the ditch terminal in *Trench 3* where a total of 66 fragments of pottery came from four separate contexts or layers. Of the 66 fragments two distinct pottery types were identified,

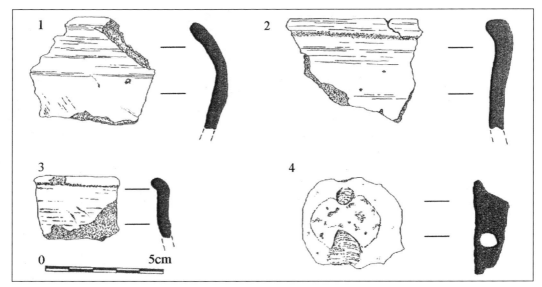

Figure 5 Mid-late Iron Age finds from the ditch fill in Trench 3.
(© Herefordshire Archaeology)
1. Handmade jar of Malvernian metamorphic Group A with linear pattern and
burnishing, typical of the late Iron Age.
2. Handmade jar of Mudstone tempered ware, Group D, with a slightly beaded rim.
3. Handmade jar of Mudstone tempered ware, Group D, fragment from a near-upright
jar with a slightly lipped rim. Traces of linear pattern and burnishing, typical of late
Iron Age.
4. An abraded lug, apparently sheared from the rest of the vessel suggesting it was
applied separately. Probably from the side of a vessel, the hole being suitable for the jar
to be suspended by hooks or twine.

consisting of a Malvernian metamorphic fabric and a Mudstone tempered ware associated with the Middle (*c.*300–100 BC) to Late Iron Age (*c.*100 BC–50 AD).

In addition to the assemblage from *Trench 3*, a single fragment of Mudstone tempered ware was excavated in *Trench 1*. This was recovered from within a compacted clay horizon identified as the interior surface of an oval or circular structure or building. The walls of the structure were set into a foundation cut that was packed with stone to support timber posts. The building would have been constructed of timber and wattle and daub with a straw or thatch roof. The entrance to the building was north facing and measured 1m wide, the approach to which had a stone pavement which had slumped to form a hollow through use. Excavation within the interior of the structure indicated that there may have been two phases of occupation. These separate phases were marked by the discovery of two layers of compacted clay flooring, both of which contained a high concentration of charcoal inclusions. The presence of charcoal in clear association with both floor levels indicates the presence of fire suggesting some form of domestic or industrial structure. In addition to these features, a possible rubbish pit was discovered to the east of the oval/circular building measuring 1m diameter; its depth and content is unknown as it was not fully excavated.

The results of *Trench 2* indicated that upon completion of the enclosure, the ditch had a maximum depth of almost 1.5m and was 2m wide, with a 'U'-shaped profile. It had been cut into the sandstone bedrock' the resulting stone being used in the construction of the bank. The sequence of ditch fills recorded indicate that it had been allowed to silt up prior to being re-cut on at least one occasion with the possibility of a second phase of

Plate 3 Members of the community excavating the oval/sub-rectangular structure in Trench 1

silting and re-cutting before it was finally abandoned and left to fill naturally with hill-wash and material weathered from the bank.

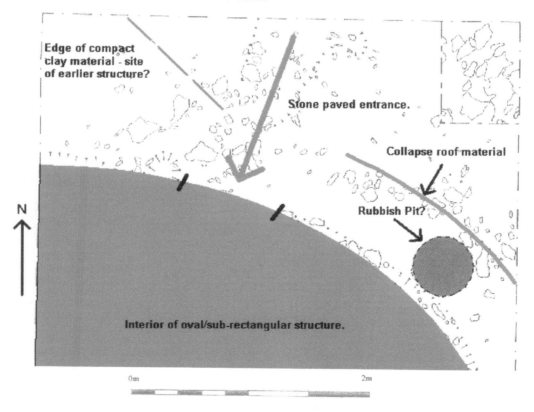

Figure 6 An interpretive plan of Trench 1. (© Herefordshire Archaeology)

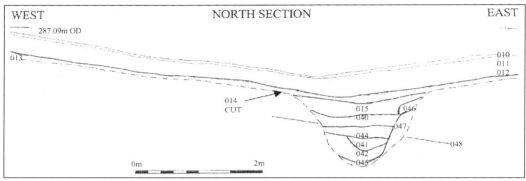

Figure 7 Section plan of 'U'-shaped ditch within Trench 2.
(© Herefordshire Archaeology)

The sequence of silting and re-cutting is within *Trench 2* is confirmed by the strati-graphic sequence recorded within the ditch terminal (*Trench 3*) to the east where it is apparent that it was re-cut at least once. It would appear that the ditch terminals, (and therefore the ditches either side of the entrance), were deliberately filled in using the stone make-up of the bank, indicating a deliberate attempt to slight the rampart on the eastern side of the enclosure. The sheer amount of stone uncovered in *Trench 3* suggests that the east-facing rampart was supported by or faced with a stone revetment which appears to be absent elsewhere along the defences. The stone-faced rampart would have been built not necessarily for protection, but as a symbol of prestige, a sight that may have been designed to impress visitors and portray an air of dominance over the surrounding landscape.

From these three small trenches, coupled with a series of detailed survey techniques, the enclosure can now be confidently attributed to the Iron Age. It would appear that it was

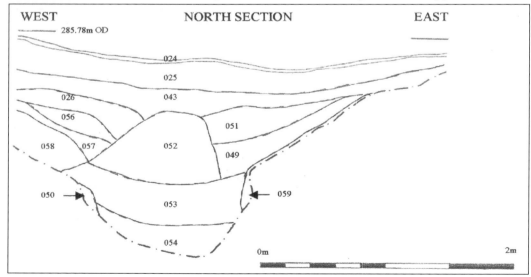

Figure 8 Section plan of the ditch terminal within Trench 3.
(© Herefordshire Archaeology)

40

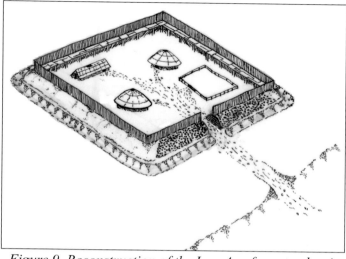

Figure 9 Reconstruction of the Iron Age farmstead as it may have appeared c.100 BC.
(© Herefordshire Archaeology)

constructed in the middle Iron Age — perhaps as early as 300 BC — and was occupied well into the late Iron Age, probably being abandoned in the first few decades AD. This would suggest that the enclosure and presumably most of Garway Hill was being utilised for over 300 years. The most likely scenario is that the enclosure represents a farmstead, lived in by an extended family unit of perhaps 20 or more individuals.

The results of the LIDAR survey over the

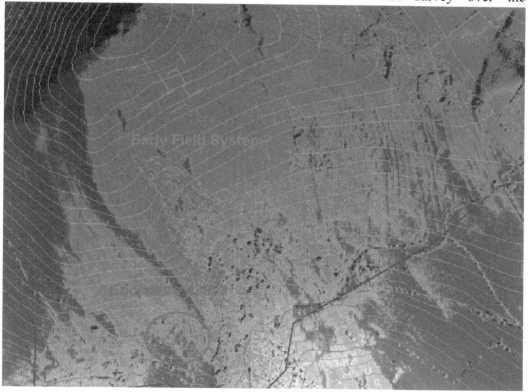

Figure 10 LIDAR results highlighting the site of the 'Celtic Fields'.
(© Herefordshire Archaeology & Environment Agency)

common indicated a possible prehistoric field system. Light Detection and Ranging (LIDAR) is an airborne mapping technique which uses a laser to accurately measure the distance between an aircraft which is carrying the equipment and the ground. This technique results in the production of a detailed three dimensional terrain map.

This field system was not visible during the ground-based survey and aerial reconnaissance due to heavy bracken cover. The area on which the field system is located lies close to the summit of Garway Hill to the south of the World War Two Radio Tracking Station site. The survey detected a number of linear anomalies that appear to interlink enclosing either square or rectangular plots of land indicative of the 'Celtic fields' that are found throughout Britain and can date from the early Bronze Age (*c*.1800 BC) through to the early medieval period. They are characterised by a patchwork of square plots rarely more than 2,000 m² in area.

Medieval use of the Common

The medieval period brought about the formation of Garway Hill Common, although at that time, (as with most common land), it was marginal land of little if any taxable value. As such it was regarded as wasteland, its main purpose being for the seasonal rough grazing of livestock. The border of the common was marked by a broad bank (2-3m wide and 1-2m high) with a deep ditch approximately 1.5m wide and 1m deep on its internal side; the internal ditch would help to prevent animals from escaping from the common and damaging crops in the surrounding fields. A funnel entrance close to the south-west corner of the common remains visible and would have once aided the herding of livestock on and off the common, interestingly a hollow way still remains to the south of this running away from the common toward the now abandoned settlement of Little Garway. This hollow way can still be traced as a modern field boundary. This route onto and off the common remained in use until at least the production of the 1st Edition Ordnance Survey (*c*.1890).

The overall size and shape of the common fluctuated greatly during the medieval period. This is best

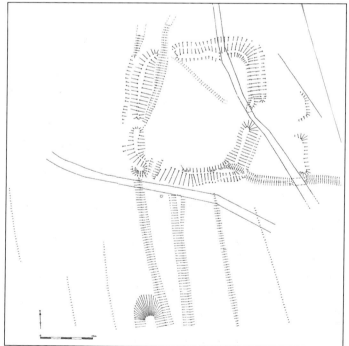

Figure 11 Medieval field boundaries to the south of the Iron Age enclosure. (© Herefordshire Archaeology)

Plate 4 Aerial observation of the medieval field boundaries to the south of the Iron Age enclosure. (© Herefordshire Archaeology & C. Musson [06-CN-0214/18])

observed within the area south of the excavated Iron Age Enclosure where two very distinct field boundary earthworks were recorded. Running from the top of the Iron Age Enclosure's south-west corner is a broad bank with a ditch on its eastern edge. This boundary runs due south and joins with the eastern edge of the funnel entrance.

To the east of this boundary, (interpreted as a demarcation boundary, which separated two land holdings), is a series of narrow linear strip fields. These are divided by a series of low banks which may have originally stood as dry-stone walls. The fields are aligned north/south, running down slope from the southern and eastern edges of the Iron Age enclosure. To the west of the demarcation boundary a series of north/south aligned terraces survive running down slope from the southern edge of the main track through the common. The terraces are equally spaced approximately 14m apart and their west-facing edge stand to a height of approximately 30-60cm high.

This indicates that at some point during the medieval period the land east of the demarcation boundary was claimed or asserted from the common for agricultural purposes. In effect the demarcation boundary became the common boundary that utilised the western rampart of the Iron Age enclosure before continuing north. It was also noted during the excavation of the Iron Age enclosure that after its abandonment the interior of the enclosure was ploughed. The terraces to the west of the demarcation boundary would have been inappropriate for ploughing due to their steep gradient, instead, with the funnel entrance opening onto this area from the south it is possible that's the terraces were formed as part of an upland hay-meadow to aid the feeding of livestock.

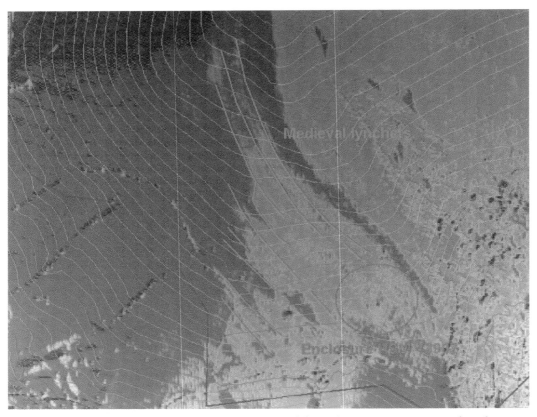

Figure 12 LIDAR results highlighting the site of the cultivation terraces within the west of the common (© Herefordshire Archaeology & Environment Agency)

Upon the west and north facing slopes of the common a major transformation took place with the formation of cultivation terraces or lynchets. They are aligned roughly north/south and vary in both length and width due to the terrain. Lynchets were constructed in order to bring into cultivation areas that would have otherwise been too steep to plough. Scattered amongst the lynchets are levelled platforms, perhaps the site of farmers' huts or storage areas. Should these features date to the medieval period they are likely to date prior to the Black Death that swept across England for the first time in 1345. Before this event Herefordshire had a population so large that it could scarcely support itself — and this in a county renowned for its agricultural production. Due to its huge population, Herefordshire farmers were driven to often extraordinary lengths in order to bring even the steepest of slopes, in the most inhospitable of environments, into cultivation. This resulted in the construction of cultivation terraces upon hillsides in a desperate attempt to feed the county's population.

During the 14th century a series of unfavourable climatic conditions closely followed by the Black Death led to a catastrophic decline in population and these marginal areas were abandoned.

Post-medieval Land-use

During the post-medieval period the most widely represented activity recorded during the survey on the common consisted of stone extraction or quarrying. The stone extracted was Old Red Sandstone which could be readily used for the construction of buildings. Quarrying was particularly prevalent within the north-western and south-western corners of the common, with smaller areas scattered elsewhere, the south-western area, known as White Rocks, being the largest extraction site. Intensive quarrying within this area has led to the formation of a re-entrant within the south-facing slope, and today sandstone blocks of considerable size remain exposed upon the surface. Within the immediate area it is possible to recognise platforms that may have supported structures associated with either seasonal accommodation for quarry workers or for storage. Further features within the area consist of levelled tracks, now overgrown with bracken, which would have once served as access to and from the quarries and led toward the now abandoned settlement of Little Garway to the south.

It is likely that the extraction of stone in the area of White Rocks began during the medieval period. The scale of the excavations may suggest that at least some of the stone quarried was used in the construction of the Church of St Michael's, Garway when it was built in 1180 replacing an earlier Saxo-Celtic church by order of the Knights Templar.

A second area of intensive stone extraction is to the north-west where again a re-entrant has formed due to quarrying into the north-facing slope. A seam of green sandstone is visible as an outcrop. Access to the quarry appears to have been from the north, either from the Kentchurch Estate or as an alternative route from the area of White Rocks and Little Garway. Like White Rocks this quarry has a number of platforms associated with it, including a hollowed track running upslope beneath the exposed sandstone seam. At the base of the slope the hollowed track joins with the track which runs parallel to the common boundary.

The remaining quarries within the common were centred on isolated spots where sandstone was visible either close to the surface or in the case of the Iron Age enclosure within an abandoned upstanding feature. A number of quarries clearly cut and disrupt earlier features indicating that these quarries are later additions to the common's history.

Changes in the Common Boundary

During the post-medieval period the size and shape of the common was altered considerably, particularly on its eastern side, where the common boundary stands as an almost straight, modern fence and planted hedge line. According to the 1840 Tithe Map of Garway Hill it is apparent the common extended to the edge of Sun lane. At a point between 1840 and the production of the 1890 1st Edition Ordnance Survey Map this land was claimed from the common to provide farmland. The land taken from the common was subsequently divided to form the rectangular fields present today. This would account for the difference in style of the modern common boundary in the east in comparison to the surviving, though eroded medieval common boundary elsewhere.

One other alteration to the boundary of the common land was observed on its western edge. Here the ruins of a cottage survive cutting the common boundary. The cottage was built using local stone and remains standing at a height of 1.2m and is aligned north/south and measures approximately 10m by 6m. The cottage consisted of at least two rooms and appears to have been one storey high and had an east-facing entrance. The site is currently overgrown with vegetation. The cottage was built astride the pre-existing common boundary which continues either side of the ruined structure to the east and west. A possible reason for this intrusion on the common lies in its close proximity to the parish of Kentchurch whereby the owners of the cottage could attempt to claim two lots of dole money under the 'poor law', claiming their occupancy lay within both parishes.

20th-century Land-use

Some of the most recent and visibly obvious features relating to 20th-century land use on the common date from the Second World War. The most imposing is the octagonal brick-built foundation for what was once a Radio Tracking Station constructed during 1942 by order of the Royal Air Force. The octagonal foundations stand approximately 2m high and the area covered measures roughly 10m diameter. Outside of the structure, set at each corner, is a concrete foundation used to house supports for what was once an upstanding timber-built tower above the surviving brick foundations. The brick foundations of the

Plate 5 Aerial coverage of the Radio Tracking Station and Barrack Block viewed from northeast. (© Herefordshire Archaeology & C. Musson. [06-CN-0313/14])

Radio Tracking Station sit centrally to a 30m-square area enclosed by a bank and ditch circuit which was constructed as a firebreak.

Associated with the Radio Tracking Station were two further structures still visible today as rectangular concrete foundations with some brick visible either as part of the foundations or as collapsed scattered material. To the north-east of the Radio Tracking Station are the remains of the Barrack Block enclosed within an area 30m-square bank and ditch firebreak. The site today is waterlogged on its southern half due to a neighbouring spring. The rectangular foundations survive as concrete with brick lining around its edges. The remains suggest that the structure had two rooms and was single storey, a band of power cables protrude from the foundation's northern edge indicating that the site was once powered. Both the Radio Tracking Station and Barrack Block were powered by a generator sited along the edge of the common to the north-east. The building which housed the generator survives as a brick lined rectangular concrete foundation with scattered brick upon the interior.

Conclusion

The results of the project illustrate that Garway Hill Common has a rich and diverse historical and archaeological resource. A basic phasing of archaeological features upon the common can be made to establish a chronological sequence. The majority of information obtained during the project resulted from a series of walkover surveys of the common. Archaeological features were recorded using a handheld Global Positioning by Satellite unit (GPS) and the information transferred onto a database to produce a point-data map from which the Herefordshire Sites and Monument Recorded could be updated.

Combining the walkover survey results with that of the LIDAR and aerial photography, provided evidence for possible prehistoric settlement and farming. The suite of archaeological techniques employed during the project led to the dating of the large enclosure together with a detailed understanding of changes in land use and population over the last three millennia. By including the LIDAR survey, a possible area for an early field system or 'Celtic field' system was identified. This series of subtle features would otherwise have been missed completely.

The majority of the field survey information recorded during this project relates to the medieval and post-medieval periods. It is clear that the medieval period saw the re-introduction, (post Iron Age), of the intensive use of the common for agricultural purposes both for intensive arable cultivation, (ploughing), and for the grazing of livestock. It was with the post-medieval period that industrial activity became more apparent, in particular quarrying. It was at this time that the vast quarry at White Rocks appeared. Though quarrying was clearly a major industry on the common land, the use of the land for grazing continued. This was also a period that saw the overall size of the common change to what it is today, this is particularly so in the east where the common boundary can be observed as a modern fence and hedgerow. During the medieval period the common had extended further east, up to the edge of Sun lane. At some point after the production of the 1840 Tithe map this land had been cut out from the common to produce the modern rectangular fields visible today.

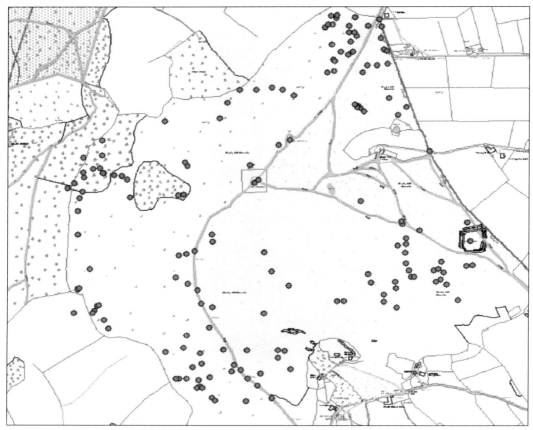

Figure 13 Scale 1:7000 map of Garway Hill Common including each site recorded during the walkover survey. (© Herefordshire Archaeology)

The most recent archaeology to be recorded upon the common came from the Second World War sites and the few 'shell scrapes' that surround the area. Of the three sites, the Radio Tracking Station was the most visually striking, followed by the foundations of the barrack block and generator block.

This community project, although small in scale, has effectively re-written the historical development of Garway Hill Common. Evidence of its prehistoric past has long been assumed and supposed, due to the chance finds of flint artefacts. However, there is now incontrovertible evidence that Garway Hill was farmed and settled during the mid to late Iron Age and that this piece of marginal land played a major role in helping to sustain the surrounding community during the early Medieval period. During the post-medieval period the common saw the introduction of quarrying on an industrial scale. During the Second World War its topography and location made it an important military radio station. Today Garway Hill Common is being actively preserved as common land by the Commoners Association and surrounding landowners for the continued enjoyment of both local people and visitors from farther afield.

5 ON GARWAY HILL ·

On Garway Hill the bracken green
Grows tall enough to form a screen
And there I have my secret shrine ·
Beyond the fringe of ragged pine
The upland thyme with purple sheen
Carpets my sanctuary between
The furze and bracken, where the keen
Sweet scents are incense all divine
      On Garway Hill ·
There is my church, a vast demesne,
From whence I view a glorious scene,
No boundaries my soul confine,
All food is holy bread and wine,
No dogma dims the joy I glean
      On Garway Hill ·

'On Garway Hill', by Lettie Cole

Lettie Cole was born in Pontrilas at the end of the 19th century. She was a daughter of John and Jean Cole who owned the village stores in Victorian times. Her nephew, John Cole, was the third generation to run the business which was finally closed in 1999 after over a hundred years of service.

After she died a notebook was found entitled, 'War Poems and Other Verse', by Lettie Cole and dedicated, For Mother. The earliest poem is dated 1911; the last written in 1972, is a sonnet entitled To Myself on My Birthday.

Lettie wrote most of the poems during the First World War with titles such as Mothers of Soldiers, the Trenches, Last Leave. It would seem that she entered poetry competitions as there are footnotes, one reading 'Girl's Own Paper 1913' and another 'Abergavenny Eisteddford, Recitation Competition, 1920'. Her poem, 'The Song of the Bread Cart Girl', was written in 1917. She obviously had a great love of the countryside and wildlife as is voiced in her poems, 'On Garway Hill' (1916) and 'A Song of Three Hills' (1925).

A SONG OF THREE HILLS

When you have climbed on Saddlebow
    You see across the land
The hills and vales with farmsteads neat,
And patchwork slopes that go to meet
The stately mountains' naked feet.
    Where they, the out-posts, stand ——

    You catch a glimpse of Hereford,
        You mark the bounds of Wales,
    The bracken covered banks that go
    To Kilpeck nestling down below.
    When you have climbed on Saddlebow
        By faint and lonely trails.

When you have climbed up Garway Hill
The country that you see
Is Heaven beneath a thin disguise:
(The Sugar-loaf and Skirrid rise
To guard the fields of Paradise,
Or so it seems to me)——

You see the valley of the Dore,
You see the Monnow wend
Its course along by weir and mill
In silver ripples never still,
When you have climbed up Garway Hill
The hill that is my friend.

But when you climb upon the Graig
Above old Grosmont town,
Along a fir-lit avenue
Of whisp'ring pines you find a view
That fills the very soul of you,
A glory and a crown!

O, sing unto the listening clouds,
Shout to the wind with me!
For here you can your joy renew,
Here you can see with other few
Far, far away a flash of blue
They tell me is the sea!

THE SONG OF THE BREAD-CART GIRL.

While all the men are away at war
   The girls must do their best
To carry on in England for
   Their loyalty's at test,
And some of the work must still be done,
   The people must be fed,
So I drive a van, to release a man,
   Delivering bread.

The work's the same, day in, day out
   (As work is apt to be),
But when there's ice or snow about
   There's no monotony!
If 'travelling's bad' and the horses slip,
   And you fall out on your head —
That's the fun that happens to one
   Delivering bread!

I'll stick to my work from first to last,
   I don't believe in strikes,
But when the war is over and past
   Anyone who likes
Can come and apply for a bread-cart job
   And do it in my stead,
And after the war for me no more
   Delivering bread!

Chorus:

Oh! its down to Orcop and up to the Globe
   And up and down the lane,
Past the Pigeon House, through the ruts,
   And up the hill again —
Or its through Ewyas Harold to Dulas Lodge
   And off to Abbeydore,
By the Bwtches to Normbridge Church
   Then turn for home once more —
In frost or snow, when cold winds blow,
   When the sun shines overhead,
At ten I start in my old white cart
   Delivering bread!

52

6   Fauna and Flora of the Common

Garway Hill common covers an area of 85 hectares (just over 200 acres) and rises to a height of 1,200 feet. The common is largely covered with continuous bracken (*Pteridium aquilinum*), beneath which there is still an extensive ground layer of grassland vegetation. This plant community, of which heath bedstraw (*Galium saxatile*), tormentil (*Potentilla erecta*), common bent grass (*Agrostis capillaris*) and sheep's fescue (*Festuca ovina*) are all good indicators, is known as acid grassland due to its tendency to prefer soils that are slightly acidic. It is a habitat that is now far less widespread than it would have been a hundred years ago. Commons, with their traditional patterns of management, have avoided being ploughed, fertilized and re-seeded and now form important havens of acid grassland within the county.

On many commons grazing levels have reduced in recent years, giving bracken the opportunity to become increasingly dominant. As well as shading out the vegetation trying to grow beneath it, dead bracken litter can build up forming layers that eventually choke out the various species that make up the acid grassland community. It is hoped that a programme of cutting and rolling of bracken starting in the summer of 2007 will reduce its vigour, thus allowing the acid grassland to thrive.

Ponies on Garway Hill

Meadow Saffron (*Colchicum autumnale*)

Bluebells (*Hyacinthoides non-scriptus*) give the common their characteristically beautiful hue in April and May. Although widespread in Britain, this species is less common elsewhere in Europe, making the UK a stronghold for this species. Mistletoe (*Viscum album*) which grows on a number of the trees on the common is a Herefordshire speciality. Another such speciality which grows on Garway Hill is meadow saffron (*Colchicum autumnale*). This has striking pink flowers appearing towards the end of summer. It is believed that this may have been planted in the past so that it could be harvested and used in the dyeing of cloth. Herefordshire is at the core of its rather limited national distribution.

In spring the surface of the Black Pool on the common is dotted with the beautiful delicate white flowers of water crowfoot (*Ranunculus aquaticus*). A number of springs emerge on the sides of the common and as they run downhill produce linear wet flushes of vegetation, providing a habitat for another member of the buttercup family, lesser spearwort (*Ranunculus flammula*). Other species preferring these damper environments include water mint (*Mentha aquatica*) and brooklime (*Veronica beccabunga*). In June 2005, Herefordshire Botanical Society recorded the stonewort (*Chara globularis*) growing in one of the wet flushes on the common. It is believed that this is the first time that this species has been recorded in Herefordshire in recent years.

As well as being of particular botanical interest, the wet flushes on the common are also of note for their fauna. For example the quality of the assemblage of water beetle species is high, with *Hyroporus discretus* only having been recorded in one other location in the county.

When the largest wet flush, on the north-western side of the common, was surveyed in August 2005, another rarity was discovered. This is a tiny mollusc called the mud snail *Lymnaea glabra.* The mud snail is included in the Red Data Book for Invertebrates (other than insects), Red Data species being those 'whose survival in Great Britain is considered under threat'. The mud snail has become extinct over large parts of lowland England and shows a continuing decline. It tends to occur in small muddy pools and ditches on ancient uncultivated land such as heaths and commons.

The Black Pool is also of considerable interest for its fauna. In August 2005 all three species of British newt were recorded in the pool: the great crested newt, smooth newt and palmate newt. The great crested newt is very highly protected and again Herefordshire is a stronghold for this species.

The Black Pool is used as a source of drinking water for the ponies grazing on the common which has caused some erosion of the pond edges. To reduce this and to provide cover for newts leaving and entering the pond, it is planned to plant a line of gorse bushes along one side of the pool. It is also proposed to build a couple of 'newt hibernacula'. These are small pits filled with rubble. It is hoped that the gaps between the rubble will provide safe, secure places in which the newts can hibernate.

In the spring of 2007 surveys for reptiles were carried out. Grass snakes have been sighted in gardens surrounding the common and it is likely that these move across the common in the late Spring and Summer months when the bracken has grown dense. Slow worms have also been recorded in gardens and these are likely to be fairly well distributed around the common. Although resembling a snake, these are in fact legless lizards.

Recent survey work has so far failed to locate any adders on the common. In fact we are not aware of any sightings in the area for at least ten years. In his book of 1901, *The Life History of British Serpents*, Leighton devoted a whole chapter to Garway Hill. He claimed that adders reached a larger than average size here and were relatively common. It is likely that factors such as persecution by gamekeepers on neighbouring estates and heavy grazing on the common have lead to its extinction. One hundred years ago, Leighton found adders but not grass snakes, now the reverse is true.

Glow-worms have been seen in the White Rocks area of the common, where the larvae hibernate under rocks or in log piles. The best time to see them is from about 10.30pm onwards from 25 June to 15 July.

John Partridge, the County Arachnological Recorder, conducted a survey for spiders in August 2005, in which 13 species of spider were recorded.

The common supports a number of anthills of the yellow meadow ant (*Lasius flavus*). It is likely that these will be providing a food source for the green woodpecker.

The Birds of Garway Hill

Garway Hill has a good variety of habitat for birds including patches of gorse, short turf, areas of trees and grassland, wetter areas around out-flowing springs and an area of more mature trees with holes. However the largest area is bracken which covers 87% of the common — with only 5% grassland. The bracken, until recent years, was regularly used for animal bedding while other areas of bracken were swiped (cut and rolled) to encourage grass growth to maintain better grazing.

Garway Hill is rarely mentioned in earlier bird books on Herefordshire. Bull (1888) writes, (according to a Mr Lingwood), of a Great Grey Shrike as occurring at Garway.

Horne (1889) notes that a specimen of the Rose coloured Starling in Hereford Museum is labelled 'Garway 1885'. Watkins (1898) in *Birds of a Herefordshire Parish* noted that until about 1886 ravens nested on Garway Hill and that keepers probably shot the last pair that bred in Herefordshire. Walker and Smith (1975) state that stonechats had bred on the upland commons of Garway and Orcop, but that they had vanished after the great frost of 1947.They would be pleased to know that stonechats have returned to breed again — in 2006 there were two breeding pairs on the Hill. Nightingales could be heard singing in Burnt Wood up until the 1950s. In 1994 Paul Scrivens led a group of bird ringers in the White Rocks area of the common. He remarked how difficult it was to catch even the most common of breeding birds and only 49 birds of 12 species were caught. The only unusual bird was a siskin feeding on ivy berries.

Garway Hill has a breeding record of 51 species, of which 11 are Birds of Conservation Concern (BCC) Red List birds: skylark, song thrush, grasshopper warbler, spotted flycatcher, marsh tit, willow tit, starling, house sparrow, linnet, bullfinch and yellow hammer. There are 13 BCC Amber List species — including cuckoo, tree pipit, redstart and stonechat. The Hill is a good area for raptors and sparrow hawk, common buzzard, kestrel, and peregrine are frequently recorded. Red kites are also recorded regularly and hobbies are seen in summer attacking the house martin flock. Both long-eared owls and short-eared owls have been recorded. In winter, flocks of redwing and fieldfare regularly feed on the many hawthorn berries, small flocks of siskin and crossbill are seen on the woodland fringe, and migrant woodcock join resident ones in the damper areas.

Flocks of migrating birds are regularly recorded in season, especially passerines, waders and wood pigeons. In most years wheatears are reported as being present for a few days, usually in spring. Occasionally rarities have occurred, such as a long-eared owl in May 1994, golden oriole in July 1997, grasshopper warbler in 1997, 1998 and 2000 and water rail in December 1997. In the summer months a walk on Garway Hill will quickly make you aware of meadow pipit and skylark using the short grassy areas, and with careful searching willow warbler, redstart and tree pipit can be found on the woodland fringe; and stonechat, yellow hammer and linnet amongst the gorse and bracken. Since the 'Foot and Mouth' outbreak in 2001 the number of grazing animals, mainly sheep, have been greatly reduced and as a result the encroachment of bracken has been greater. The recently published Commons Management Plan will help redress the balance by cutting the bracken so increasing the grass area, planting hedges along the boundary, planting berry-bearing shrubs and the putting up of nest boxes for breeding birds, especially to encourage pied flycatchers.

Birds seen on the common from April to September in 2006 were: pheasant, buzzard, kestrel, peregrine, stock dove, wood pigeon, collared dove, cuckoo green wood pecker, skylark, swallow, house martin, tree pipit, meadow pipit, pied wagtail, wren, dunnock, robin, redstart, stonechat, blackbird, song thrush, mistle thrush, blackcap, garden warbler, whitethroat, chiffchaff, willow warbler, goldcrest, spotted flycatcher, long-tailed tit, blue tit, great tit, coal tit, nuthatch, jay, magpie, carrion crow, raven, starling, house sparrow, chaffinch, greenfinch, goldfinch, linnet, bullfinch and yellow hammer.

7   Coal, Clogs and Catastrophe

The once heavily wooded slopes of Garway Hill have been eroded, albeit very slowly, by various industries that needed timber as an energy source. Even the local bowmen, retainers of John Scudamore in the 1400s, would have been fashioning their longbows out of these very woods. Border warfare was at it height around this period and a constant supply of arms was necessary for the frequent skirmishes between Scudamores and Abrahalls against the might of the Talbots. Who knows how many ships that sailed the oceans have been built with the help of oak timber requisitioned from the Kentchurch woods?

One of the earliest occupations to need a constant supply of wood was that of the charcoal maker. Charcoal was made in large quantities for both domestic use and the smelting of ore, from at least Roman times. There is no evidence to support this early usage around Garway Hill, although the area around Court-a-Grove farm has Roman pottery sherd finds from the 2nd to 4th centuries. Field names with the word 'Colliers' are indicative of places where these craftsmen may have plied their trade in more recent times, and there are two in Kentchurch parish mentioned in the Tithe Maps — Great and Little Colliers — both owned by a William Matthews, along with a Colliers Orles at Old Hall in Orcop owned by Thomas George Symons Esq.

The making of charcoal is an age old craft which came into its own as the fuel used for creating the high temperatures needed for smelting ores, particularly iron, and also for the burning of lime. The wood chosen for use was usually cut the previous winter, between September and March, and then stacked in the woods in the form of cords. A cord was a stack of specified dimensions but these varied in size and volume between regions. It is said that the use of heavy hardwoods such as a beech was best, but oak, elm or ash were left for their timber and it was usually only the pollarded and lopped branches of these quality trees that the wood collier would use. The itinerant workers were usually at a site for a month or two during the summer season, and built themselves short-term shelters out of wood and turf, where they would live while they worked. Wooden poles, about 15 feet long and 10 inches in diameter, were placed in a circle then securely tied at the top. This structure was covered with brushwood and then turfs, grass side inwards, which were laid overlapping from the base upwards. A 'door' might be made of planks or short poles that were tied together. In more modern times canvas and tarpaulin 'tents' were used instead, being much more convenient.

The ideal size wood to use for burning was that with a diameter between two and five inches, so a method of coppicing was used to ensure a continuous supply. One acre of fast growing coppice wood such as alder, ash, birch or hazel would produce a supply every 16 to 17 years, whereas coppice rotation on beech could be 20 years or more. Coppice wood was also used to make handles for tools; hoops for barrels and even the twigs could be used for

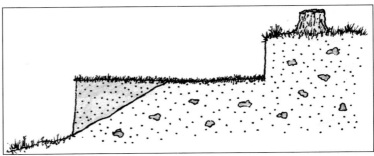

A diagrammatic picture of the construction of a charcoal platform on the hillside

besom making. The 1851 Census for Orcop parish includes two coopers, a basket maker, a besom maker and a white hoop maker as well as carpenters, sawyers and woodmen.

A site was chosen for the charcoal platform, ideally on level, well drained ground, sheltered from high winds and near a water source. On land that sloped a method called 'cut-and-fill' was used to create a working surface, known locally as a hearth, level, flat or pit. To have a good base, or floor, was essential and sites were often re-used, especially as it was claimed that where wood had been coaled before you got a better yield of charcoal. A nearby water supply was essential, not only to save on labour but for emergencies. Flames from an out of control stack could soon set the whole woodland alight. Some men worked alone but continuous attention to the stack, both day and night, made it a far easier job for two or more. If the wind suddenly got up or changed direction a frantic movement of adjustable screens was necessary. These were hurdles made out of ash or hazel about eight feet by six feet in size and could be moved around the stack to provide shelter from the prevailing wind. They were usually placed quite close to the burn, inclining over them to ensure maximum shelter. Sometimes bracken or furze piled up against the screen was used as an additional buffer.

The most commonly used method for charcoal burning was to make circular piles. Records from the mediaeval period show that these could be from 20 to 30 feet across but more modern ones were smaller, being between 12 to 16 feet. The method of stacking the wood varied around the regions but the basic idea was to construct a pile of wood, perhaps about nine feet in height, covering it with a surface of overlapping turf, grass side inwards, that would seal it against the air outside. Using green bracken or straw and then turf and earth was another method. Some small vents were purposely left, by which the rate of charring could be adjusted. By opening or closing these dampers it was possible to provide either more or less ventilation. The stack was lit by either dropping charcoal or dry sticks down a carefully created central chimney followed by shovels full of burning wood or 'coals that are fully kindled'. The top was then made completely airtight with turf and sealed with earth. The duration of the burn could be anything from two to nine days dependant on its size, wind conditions and the moisture content of the wood. The stack was extinguished by completely blocking off all vents and damping down with water, if deemed necessary. The turf covering was then raked off, any partially charred wood set aside to be used again and the charcoal lumps bagged ready to be transported by pack-horse, mule or donkey, to its destination.

The 16th century saw a significant rise in the demand for charcoal with the introduction of the blast furnace and power forge. There was also a need for sufficient large timber to remain for construction work and shipbuilding. In 1558 an Act was passed to prohibit the felling for charcoal production of ash, beech and oak, one foot wide at the stub, which grew within 14 miles of the sea or any river navigable from the sea, although exceptions were made and special licences granted. The rivers Wye and Severn were both specified by name. This legislation certainly helped to prevent the wholesale destruction of the ancient forests. Records indicate at least four tons of charcoal are needed to smelt enough iron ore for one ton of pig iron and a further three tons of charcoal to convert this pig iron to wrought iron.

Post-medieval charcoal burning platforms have been found in Kentchurch Deer Park, Copse Wood and Burnt House Wood. On the opposite side of the hill there is certainly evidence of charcoal making activity although from which century it is hard to determine. Black Pitts Farm, as the land was known in earlier times, had all the requisites necessary, including a good water supply and the woodland still has evidence of being coppiced. In recent years, when pigs were being kept on the land and were rooting in the earth, the combination of a hot sunny day and heavy rainfall would produce a smell in the air that could only be described as 'wet soot'. In places below the surface the ground is still littered with charcoal, which perhaps gave rise to the name 'Black Pitts'. A nearby field still has the remains of an old sawpit.

Clog making is a craft that has almost completely disappeared nowadays, the art and skill involved being seen mostly at demonstration events. This activity was still taking place at Kentchurch up until the 1900s. A local place name in the area is 'Cobblers Grove'. In the middle ages clogs were worn by both rich and poor, but in later years mostly by factory workers, miners and those who worked on the land, especially in the north of England and Wales. There were two differing types of clog makers, the local village craftsman or the itinerant cloggers who worked in gangs travelling the countryside. Whereas the local man in the village would take precise measurements of each foot, shape a pattern and then cut the clog soles accordingly, the itinerant worker only made rough cut outs. The greenwood of alder, birch, beech or sycamore was chosen, but traditionally the itinerant clogger favoured alder, which would only be harvested in the spring and summer months making this very much a seasonal occupation. When grown under suitable conditions, with constant moisture to its roots, ideally alongside streams or rivers, this wood was extremely durable. Sycamore was also popular in Wales and could be felled all year round. The itinerant workers would move from one grove to another, erecting temporary shelters as they went. Trees with a girth of no more than two feet were selected, felled and then cut into logs of a fixed length — man, woman, child and 'between'. The 'trimmings' and waste material were often sold as pea sticks and firewood to earn them extra money. The logs were then split into blocks and cut to rough shape with a side-axe, then, using a knife, pared to shape the heel and sole. As this 'breaking up' process was done whilst the wood was still green and moist, the clog blocks then had to be allowed to dry out. They were

layered in small conical stacks, arranged in such a way that the air could freely circulate to facilitate the drying process. This could last for weeks or even months, dependant upon the quality of wood and weather conditions. These rough hewn blocks were then sold on to the clogging factories in places like Lancashire and Yorkshire where they would be 'fine-pared' and the leather uppers added by nailing on with short flat headed nails. Grooved irons would be nailed to the heel and sole and a copper or brass tip tacked on to the front. A pair of clogs could last for many years if worn nails were replaced. Wales and the borders were particularly popular with these travelling gangs but they were a common sight in most parts of Britain before the outbreak of the Second World War.

Cloggers at work at Kentchurch in the late 1800s, early 1900s. The lower photograph shows clog blocks stacked and airing

The woods of Kentchurch Park once belonged to the Knights Hospitaller but were confiscated at the Reformation and in 1547 were sold to John Scudamore of Nuneham Courtenay. At that time they comprised 250 acres and contained about 130 fallow deer. This ancient woodland held much fine and valuable timber, not least a plentiful supply of oaks, one of which, a pedunculate oak, is known as Jack of Kent's oak. Its girth was measured at 37 feet 3 inches in 1991 and its age is estimated at around 970 years. A well established yew on the estate is indicated on modern Ordnance Survey maps. In 1823 a valuation of £3,895 was placed on 378 oak trees offered for sale with the comment, 'as fine naval timber as ever was sent out of the county'. Kentchurch oaks were still being sent to the Royal Naval dockyard at Deptford in 1826.

The tiny hamlet of Bagwyllydiart at one time would have been no more than a small clearing in the woods, a place where the four parishes of Garway, Kentchurch, Kilpeck and Orcop came together and trackways through the wooded areas crossed. In earlier times it would have been of some importance as crossroads at parish boundaries were significant meeting places where markets were often held. In 1814 the Bagwyllydiart Estate amounted to just over 52 acres, most of this still woodland, but there was revenue to be generated by the sale of timber. In 1840, John Herbert, The Garth, Monmouthshire,

Timber hauling at Bagwyllydiart in the early 1900s

proposed to cut down 60 oaks on this estate to which John Lucas Scudamore was entitled to one third of the proceeds as Lord of the Manor. Nowadays there is a handful of houses with the trees all but gone.

In 1984 York Minster was severely damaged by fire and a nationwide appeal was made to donate oaks for its restoration. The Foxley, Mansel Lacy and Kentchurch estates responded by each offering to sacrifice one of their fine oaks. Local haulier Maurice Duggan provided the transport to their destination free of charge. Each tree was said to be about 150 years old and estimated to provide around 200 cubic feet of timber.

In May 1959 a tragedy almost happened during logging timber from the estate. Temperatures had been high in the early part of the month, which gave rise to a series of thunderstorms. Reports from around the county showed cattle being killed by lightning, buildings and trees struck and hay destroyed by fire as well as severe flooding. On Tuesday, 12 May, the rainfall was particularly heavy and some who remember this occasion say that it was a 'cloud burst' over Garway Hill that caused the particular problems that followed. Down in Kentchurch Deer Park, on ground already sodden, the force of water began to run down the surface of the land taking all before it. Logs and brushwood left after timber felling, began washing down the hill towards the Bannut Tree Farm. Here, the swollen stream carried the debris onwards until wedged logs and branches began forming a natural dam, causing the ever-increasing water to build up behind it. In no time at all the pressure had built to such an extent that it burst through, racing on down the hillside. Newly planted rhododendron bushes in the Court shrubbery added to the raging and swirling flow and before long another dam had been formed by the build up of the debris against the small stone bridge where the shrubbery bordered the lawns of the house. An uprooted oak tree added to the chaos and with nowhere else to go the stream was effectively diverted across the lawns towards the house. These lawns, being slightly lower than the surrounding land caused a lake to be formed until the increasing pressure eventually forced the water into the kitchen. The force of the water was severe enough to rip an Aga cooker from its fittings and carry it across the room. Internal doors broke and the water poured on through the house into the great hall. Outside, the lake was still rising by the minute and on reaching window height the enormous force of water shattered the glass and poured through to meet that already rising on the inside. Antique furniture was tossed around in the swirling torrent, some splintering and shattering beyond repair, porcelain, glass and china reduced to fragments to be found amidst the silt and rubble weeks later. Although slightly askew, after having been knocked by some of the larger furniture, the Scudamore portraits lining the great hall were left mostly intact. Fortunately, the ferocity of this wave of water was sufficient to break through the front door at the other end and out of the house and so relieve some of the pressure.

That particular evening, Lt. Commander and Lady Patricia Lucas Scudamore had not yet returned from a day out in London, whilst daughter Charlotte was away at boarding school. The nanny and two Italian servants had retired for the night and were in their rooms upstairs whilst 78-year-old Mrs Lucas-Scudamore, the Commander's mother, and her two dogs had retired to the library for the evening. Their son, young 4-year-old John, was fast asleep upstairs in bed and remained blissfully unaware of the drama that was unfolding around him.

Disturbed by the unusual noises she could hear outside the room, the elderly Mrs Lucas-Scudamore became aware of water trickling across the floor. She immediately pressed the bell to summon the butler, but before he could respond the library door suddenly gave way from the sheer pressure of water outside it and a violent surge flowed in sweeping her away with its force. After being struck by items of furniture tossing around in the maelstrom, she was eventually swept up against the library wall, where she struggled to climb on to the library Canterbury and from there to cling on to a ledge of

Kentchurch Court (© Joan Fleming Yates)

the bookcase. It was through chest-deep muddy water that the servants and nanny battled and eventually rescued both lady and dogs. The telephone, which by now was out of order, meant the only quick way that help could be summoned was to sound the fire siren. Local farmer, Mervyn Eynon, knowing this was a call for help discovered that access via the drive to the Court was blocked by water and debris but on a second attempt he managed to struggle through. On reaching the house he discovered the enormity of the situation and quickly summoned the local doctor.

Within a short while the water had begun to recede and by the time the Commander and his wife returned after midnight, at the end of a tiring day, the first sign they had of something amiss was the sight of the debris-strewn drive. After struggling through the rain and deep puddles of water they were met by Nanny, who broke the news of the scene of devastation they were about to confront. After firstly checking on the Commander's mother they straight away set about trying to rescue some of their more precious and personal treasures. They worked long in to the night and after very little sleep awoke to daylight and the harsh reality of the loss and destruction that had taken place in those few fateful hours the previous evening. It must have been a heart wrenching sight, knowing that there would be irreplaceable losses, with documents and mementos of the Scudamore history gone forever. There was, of course, one major consolation, inasmuch that there had been no loss of life.

Most of the water had now gone, leaving thick mud and rubble amidst the broken and fragmented furniture and ornaments. Such was the severity that it was to take two years to restore what was salvageable. Greenlands of Hereford transported and stored those items that could be saved and a huge garage was turned into a workshop to deal with the cleaning and repairing. Carpets and soft furnishings were constantly hosed with clean water to drive out every remnant of silt and sand; some furniture was taken to London where it required the services of specialists. Heartbreakingly, priceless documents, books and heirlooms were lost, either damaged beyond repair or swept completely away. Much had been in the family for many generations; some items brought back from trips to foreign lands, others that had been gifts or dowries. The tightly stacked books in the library, temporarily removed to the stable, were weeks later laid out in the summer sun to dry. The flooring from downstairs rooms was so warped and buckled, the water having soaked through and remained trapped underneath, that it had to be lifted and then allowed to dry naturally. It was to be two years before it was finally re-laid. Women volunteers from the neighbourhood came in on a daily basis to wash the crockery, some of which was carefully glued back together again, and hand wash the more lightly soiled soft furnishings, whilst men from the surrounding villages came to clear away the mud and other debris. Expert opinions were sought to offer advice on structural and timber damage. The smell from rotting vegetation and stagnant water trapped beneath floorboards was all pervasive. Around one hundred helpers were involved in the tasks, coming in regularly for a month and were fed hot meals by the W.R.V.S. A caravan was brought to the site, which was used as an office, kitchen and general living quarters during the day, but at night the family were able to return to the house to sleep, as the first-floor rooms remained intact. Machinery was brought in to clear the soil, stones, rotting branches and other debris that now covered the lawns, removing it, along with that from the house, up to the Deer Park. The depth of water was recorded as having reached over five feet in the front rooms and more than nine in the kitchen; in some places the silt was up to 18 inches deep. Thinking to the future, the stream was cleared and widened in the hope that it might prevent such a disaster from occurring again. Standing in the dining room alongside the plaque on the wall which reads 'The level of flood water in May, 1959' it is hard to believe, whilst looking out over the tranquil setting of the deer park, the catastrophe that unfolded in those few hours on that summer evening.

Many more houses in Kentchurch endured a similar fate, but on a lesser scale and there was no escape for houses on the other side of the hill. Those on the top road from Bagwyllydiart to Garway also suffered from a deluge of water pouring down the hill. New House, The Prospect, Dingle and Sun houses all felt the wrath of the storm and gardens were washed away.

Fred Powell surveying the damage to his and Beattie's garden at The Prospect, Garway Hill, in May 1959

Over time, the prevalence of wood and parkland around Garway Hill has made it a haven for those intent on poaching and it became almost a sport in itself for some of the locals in trying to outwit the gamekeepers. For some it was just the occasional bird or rabbit to help feed hungry mouths, for others it was a skill to be proud of. Kentchurch Estate would have been a prime target with its plentiful supply of deer and game birds that were bred especially for the large shoots that they held. Gamekeeping was a round the clock occupation seven days a week. 'You mark my words. 'Ee be up to no good, I'll be bound' was a remark made about anyone who was seen other than where they should be. Fines could be heavy and in 1787 a James Powell was fined £20 for using two dogs to kill and destroy a hare. In 1793 a Scudamore of Kentchurch Court was having problems with the local Prosser and Charles families who had taken to using nets in the Meadows Wood. After being discovered and then escaping the local Constable, he took it upon himself to deal with the matter by going to the Prossers' home at the Benarth Farm, eventually taking away dogs and nets and for which he imposed a £5 penalty. The Charles family were also causing him severe distress over the cutting and selling of timber. A postscript on the end of a letter he had written reads: 'I am so insolently treated by the Widow Charles and her Rascally Brother, I wish to punish them.' It was recorded that a certain member of the Nicholas family who farmed at Llanithog, Kentchurch, in years gone by, used to place a deer's head on the gate-post at Kentchurch Court, just to show them that he had been! There is also a record in the Estate documents relating to trouble with female poachers. One method favoured by women was to have hooks on the inside of their billowing skirts and petticoats, from which it was quite easy to hang and conceal a brace of pheasants, hare or rabbit. In the late 1800s, James Castry, from the White Rocks, Garway Hill, was notorious for his exploits and was nicknamed 'The Wild Man of the Woods'. A famous horse thief also made a hideaway at Cold Nose, now White House Farm, Orcop. David Williams, alias Deo Deliro, a clockmaker, hailed from Builth Wells but was stealing horses from as far away as Denbighshire and Somerset before secreting them deep in the wooded landscape. In 1773 Cold Nose would have been a farm not far from the edge of what was then the unenclosed common land on Garway Hill. Pugh's *Hereford Journal* of that year states:

> A singular discovery was made, it is said, last week in the Parish of Orcop, where in the middle of a thick wood a stable was found almost underground, which undoubtedly was formed for the purpose of stabling such horses as this fellow and his family might steal. For Williams regularly brought up his sons to this felonious practice. This is part of a numerous gang dispersed over the kingdom, and by exchanging horses stolen in one part of the country for those stolen in the opposite, they have for long escaped the pursuit of justice.

Not long after this, however, in September 1774, a further report includes Williams in a list of felons being transported, under guard, to plantations in America.

On the east side of the hill and what would still have been part of Garway Hill common until the Enclosure Act is an area known locally as 'The Jockies'. It was acquired by the Woodland Trust in 1998 under their scheme 'Woods on your Doorstep'. This was a Millennium project to mark the year 2000 with 200 new community woods across England and Wales. Part of the area purchased has been retained as meadow land, interspersed with old apple trees, remnants perhaps of an orchard, but the upper slopes have been planted with a variety of native broadleaved trees. These include ash, crab apple, field maple, guelder rose, hazel, oak, rowan, silver birch and wild cherry, all planted with the help of local volunteers. Bracken control was undertaken by willing volunteers who would enthusiastically go around 'bracken whacking' with long sticks or any other implement that would easily lop the heads off the new growth. A flexible car aerial proved to be an ideal tool for the job!

The woodland now also boasts a 'Holy Thorn' which was planted to replace the famous tree that used to blossom on Old Christmas Eve across the other side of the valley at Orcop Hill, but sadly is no more. We have yet to witness this spectacle with the new tree, but it is still young, and time will tell.

There are some superstitions connected with woods that are still adhered to by many locals. Burning elder wood in the house is said to be unlucky, as is bringing May blossom indoors. There are some who will not cut down Yew for fear of reprisal. In older times it was a part of normal everyday life to gather up any dead wood you might find lying around and bring it home for kindling. One of the last of his kind was the familiar figure of 'Bill Baker' who would often be seen returning to his home on Garway Hill with a bundle of firewood slung over his shoulder.

The mention of 'Fern Tickets' nowadays hardly provokes a reaction, but a few years back it would have brought a blush to many a cheek. It was often a teasing comment made to any young, or old, courting couple who had suggested a walk on the hill: ''Ave yer got yer fern ticket?' Down in the Forest of Dean, it is said that in earlier times these 'tickets' were issued only at May Day celebrations, for use that day only, and would allow the bearer to wander at will through the forest lands without having to adhere to the proper footpaths. In other words, if you haven't got a ticket, stay on the path and no sneaking off into the undergrowth!

Garway Hill and its surrounds has for various reasons over the years always attracted people to inhabit its slopes and dingles, from the hunter gatherers of the Mesolithic period 10,000 years ago and right throughout history. Whatever quality it possessed that drew those people here, nowadays it is the sheer beauty of the landscape that is the attraction. Many visitors have remarked on the special 'feel' it has and return time and again to walk to the summit and marvel over the views. Without a doubt, this border hill will have seen more turbulent times but nowadays it is enveloped with an air of peace and tranquillity and remains a special place in the hearts of many.

8   A farm on Garway Hill

Eva Whistance

Lillie Heath

Farms on Garway Hill are a mixture of large and small holdings with the hill common being important for all commoners alike, but in this study Little Garway Farm will be used as an example of farm practice on the hill in the 20th century.

Little Garway Farm was sold along with other farms on the Moore O'Farrell estate in January 1920. The purchasers were the tenants, William & Eva Whistance. It was recorded in the sale catalogue as 'a capital house stone built and tiled, very pleasantly placed containing entrance, two sitting rooms, kitchen, dairy, cellar, washhouse, four bedrooms, box room and two attics. Good garden. The premise mostly stone built includes two granaries, five and three bay wagon hovels to yard. Stable for five, chaff house, cow shed for six with range and calves' cot, engine house, two bay cart shed, implement house, four bay hovel to yard, two barns, water from a spring with tap in yard.' As the tenant, William Whistance had paid a yearly rent at Candlemas of £143 8s 6d for the 170 acres of land.

William died on 8 December 1921 aged 52, having owned the farm for under two years. Eva, his wife, born on 19 May 1874, continued to farm. She had been the local Baptist minister's daughter and married William on 23 April 1895, so it must have been a steep learning curve for her to run a farm as a widow. She did have her daughter Lillie living near by as Lillie had married Edwin Heath and was living at neighbouring Oldfield Farm.

She also had two other children: Wilfred now ten and Cuthbert seven. Daisy her eldest daughter had died in 1916 aged 18 from pneumonia and resulting complications after more than five months illness. We have a visual snapshot of her farming as Eva took her own photographs

Shropshire sheep

and developed them in the cupboard under the stairs. Emily Williams, later Mrs Lewis Powell, helped in the house and Gerry Benjamin from Hillside helped on the farm.

During World War One the Government commandeered wheat and hay, paying £20 per ton for each, to feed men and horses fighting at the Front. This continued until 1922 giving farming families a financial

Shooting rabbits in corn

Eva's Hereford cattle

Harvesting corn in Reservoir field

Binder being pulled by horses

Hedge cropping on Preigar Pitch

Emily Williams worked at Little Garway farm around 1920. Here she met and married Lewis Powell from the White Rocks

Monmouth sheep sale, September 1922

boost. In the spring of 1923, however, the government took away all food support and prices fell to £5 per ton. All other commodities were affected and the mid-'20s were grim times for farmers.

Wilfred took over the farm in 1934 when his mother died aged 60. He married Elizabeth May Bowkett in Orcop church in 1935 and over the years they had five children: Rosemary, Patrick, Prudence, Jenny and Judy and a fostered son, Gino.

According to a diary from 1938, the farm stocked 118 ewes and 104 lambs including tiddlers (orphan lambs) That year, on 29 August, 30 store lambs were sold at 26s 6d each making £39 15s at Broad Oak Livestock Sale. One ram lamb made £2 8s and a 2-year-old ram made £2 17s 6d. Five yearling heifers were sold at Broad Oak on 17 October 1938 for £10 5s each. The first beef subsidies were paid out in 1935/36. Grade A cattle received 5s per beast and grade Bs were paid 2s 6d. This continued until World War Two when the War Agricultural Committee (The War Ag) worked closely with farmers to increase production. Surprisingly Garway Hill Common was not included in cultivation plans by the War Ag, but Little Garway Farm was required to grow potatoes and sugar beet. For example two acres of both were ordered to be planted in 1942. Basic slag supplies followed and were collected from Pontrilas station having been dispatched from Ebbw Vale Steel Works. This phosphate was used to neutralise the acid in the soil and so improve the crop.

As an example of livestock prices, in June 1943, seven cattle were taken to Hereford market. After stoppages £115 10s was received for them at the auction. In October, however, the cattle trade may have dropped as five cattle made £61 8s in Ross market. At the same market 30 lambs made £97 10s. In the same year 16 ton 5 cwt of sugar beet was sold to the British Sugar Corporation at Kidderminster for £66 14s 7d. Corn was taken to E.R. Morris, The Rough, Saddlebow Common and in 1941 Mr Morris was charging 1s 3d per cwt to grind corn.

By 1946 live and dead stock is listed as 160 ewes, 165 lambs, 3 horses, 5 cows, 8 cattle (1½ years old), 7 calves, 12 pigs and 50 poultry. In the fields 9 acres were planted with mixed corn, 8½ acres of barley 20 acres of clover seed, ½ acre of potatoes and 9 acres of roots.

Horses are mentioned each year in the valuation even in the '50s. Some of these horses remain in living memory: Bonnie and Dick were important members of the farm labour force. Dick was lively and spirited as well as hard working. Every effort had to be made to keep him in at night, as he was adept at opening his stable door and field gates, and then get into neighbours' gardens and would damage their flowers and vegetables. Being temperamental when working in the shafts, he

Bonnie and Dick at the garden gate being patted by Rosemary and Patrick

would get restless and charge off with his cart or farm implement attached. When being used to collect a side rake from Taylor & Jones in Monmouth, he became fretful about the unusual cobbles beneath his hooves and pushed the side rake backwards into the large shop window, smashing the glass. One day Margaret Watkins took Dick to pull 10 cwt of corn to the mill at the Rough. All was well until Dick realised that Adams & Davy's lorry was behind him. Dick took off at speed, getting Margaret very quickly to her destination.

Horses were used in chain harrowing, ploughing, making hay, carting hay from fields, harvesting crops and carting sheaves to the barn, hoeing mangolds, taking feed out into the fields for other animals and collecting bracken off the hill. Oats were grown to feed them. They were taken to the Smithy in Garway village to be shod regularly by either Artis Ruck or his son Charlie, the blacksmiths. The Ruck family had been blacksmiths in Garway since the 1840s. Other horses were brought onto the farm for timber felling. Jack Rudge lived for several months on the farm with the horse he used to clear wood from Rocks Bottom Wood in the '40s. When Oldfield Wood was coppiced in the late '50s the horses Metal and Prince were used to pull timber on to the road. They were owned and worked by Miss Davies of Pennywink.

When crops were grown, the field needed to be ploughed, rolled and harrowed with horses. For many years the seed was planted with the horse drawn corn drill. When the crop was ready for harvesting, men using a hand hook or scythe, would cut around the headland of the field to allow the horse drawn binder to get to work. The binder would be used to cut the corn, packing the slightly unripe heads on the straw into sheaves. Men would stack the sheaves into stooks and the heads of corn would ripen. It was imperative to cut the corn just before it was fully ripened otherwise valuable grain would spill on to the ground and be wasted.

The stooks were collected and stacked in the barn to await the threshing machine, which could arrive many weeks later. Lewis Evans from Treago Farm usually came to Little Garway with his threshing machine. If he was too busy then Lance Watkins from The Lawns brought his machine which was driven by a portable steam engine. Having cut the bands, the sheaves were fed into the machine. This noisy, dusty process needed six people to assist. If the threshed corn was required for next year's seed it would be put through the winnower to extract any debris. The straw was put through the bolting tier which secured the bundle with two bands of binder twine. Later this was put into a rick and thatched to protect it from the winter storms.

Hay making was equally back breaking work. Horses pulled a mowing machine to cut the grass. It was then teased out

Horses Bonnie and Dick in the hay field with Rosemary and friend

and turned by lots of willing helpers using rakes and pikes. When the grass was dry it was collected on a horse drawn hay wagon, taken to the hayrick and pitched up to form a large stack. Friends and neighbours helped out with all this work. And they in turn needed refreshments. Large jugs of tea, with wicker baskets full of sandwiches and cakes were taken to the hay fields at lunch and teatime. The hayrick was soon thatched to protect it against the elements. A large very sharp hay knife was used to cut quantities for the livestock to eat every day throughout the winter months.

All of this hard manual work was rewarded with the occasional swig of cider to quench the thirst. At Little Garway Farm Sid Benjamin would make the 150 gallons of perry and cider each year. He was employed by Len Francis to take a travelling cider scratter and press around farms. Once the cider had fermented in the barrels Sid would come and sample it before it was corked down. Cider played its part in the hospitality enjoyed at Little Garway Farm.

A break for a photograph during thistle cutting — Patrick, Prudence and Geoff Powell

Hedging, ditching, thistle cutting, and stone picking were all needed to sustain the fields. When all of the harvesting was finished, the farm workers took up their hedge bills and cut the hedges. Collecting the cuttings they would ferry them back to the farm and cover the mangold heap to help protect against frost. Thistle cutting was a job the children

Gordon Barrell and Idris Morgan combining in the 1960s at Church farm, Garway

72

were asked to do in their summer holidays. Wilf found it was best to put each child in a field on their own as if they were together too much talking and too little cutting took place.

Gradually, during the '30s, '40s and '50s some machinery found its way onto the hill to replace horsepower. Eddie Heath from Oldfield bought the first tractor on the hill in 1939. It was an Alice Chalmers B.; Jack had a half day off school to see it arrive and subsequently he would run home from school to drive it, pulling a single furrow plough. A pitcher, or a hay loader, could be seen on some farms towed at the back of the horse drawn cart to elevate the hay on to the cart. Mobile bailers came in the late '40s. The first hedge cutters came along in the late '50s and were like mowing machines but stronger. At Little Garway Farm in the '40s they had a Fordson tractor with spade lugs on steel wheels which helped on the steep banks. Several frightening stories are told about tractors going out of control on such banks at Little Garway. On one occasion Ted Jones and Tony Smith were taking a tractor down the Windells banks when the weight of the trailer pushing behind, tipped the tractor over. Mervyn Eynon of Pontrilas, Ernie Francis of Garway and Lewis Evans of Treago, had tractor driven combine harvesters in the early '60s.

Beet harvesting did not become mechanised until the late '40s. As the war effort included beet growing, lots of manual labour was required. When it was ready for harvesting the rows of beet were pulled by hand, after being loosened by a single furrow plough, knocked together to remove soil and left in rows to wilt. Next the leaves were removed with a beet chopper and the beet was put in heaps. Then the beet was loaded onto a horse drawn cart and taken to the roadside. Here it was put on a lorry and taken to Pontrilas station. Four lorry loads were needed to fill a railway truck which the shunters had lined up in a siding ready for filling.

Harvesting activities brought the farmers' attention to the damage done to crops by rabbits. Jack Heath remembers a group of gypsies helping with the harvest in a 3-acre field. Their lurcher dogs caught 105 rabbits in one afternoon. Tony Smith used ferrets, long nets and a gun to bag his rabbits on the hill and Tony remembers catching 100 rabbits, assisted by his brother, in one weekend. A butcher would come up from Nelson in Mid Glamorgan and buy rabbits at the Globe pub. Tony remembers prices fluctuating from 2s to 3s 6d during the war years. Ernie Francis remembers Mr Stannaforth buying damsons, pigeons and rabbits throughout the war, and relied on money from his rabbit catching to finance his weekend entertainment. Mrs Eva Smith from Old Kitchen Farm also bought farm produce and took it to sell on her stall in The Butter Market in Hereford. In 1955 myxomatosis reached Garway Hill and soon the rabbit population was decimated and the sluggish, swollen eyed rabbits could be seen suffering a hideous and slow death in the hedgerows and on the roads.

Garway Hill's topography dictates livestock rearing on farms rather than the growing of arable crops. Some fields are so steep that only horses, not tractors, could be used on them. Garway Hill livestock has long been sought after. In the 1930s a buyer from the Pennines would visit farms to purchase store cattle. Consequently Oldfield stock, along with other local cattle, was walked to Pontrilas to be transported by rail to Derby. Ewyas Harold (Temple Bar Car park) and Broad Oak markets were used to sell store animals to other farms. During the war Chadwick auctioneers held regular fatstock markets at Ewyas Harold, whereas Broad Oak was always a store market with two auctions in the spring and two in the autumn, run by Coles, Knapp and Kennedy. Wilf used his Ford van to convey sheep and calves to market. Unfortunately the van had very poor brakes and so, when on holiday from school, Patrick's help was needed to hold the hand brake on when going down the Spite House Pitch to Ewyas Harold market. The Ford van was replaced by a Standard Vanguard model, which also allowed the family to go out together for outings. Mr Bert Gardiner also transported cattle to market. In June 1943 he charged £1 to convey seven cattle to Hereford market from Little Garway Farm.

Ewes were lambed outside and checked in the night using the light of hurricane lamps. When the lambs were 6 weeks old their tails were chopped and the male lambs were castrated using pinchers referred to as 'the bloodless'. Mintic powder was used to drench lambs for worms. Water was added and measured to suit the lamb's weight. Two fluid ounces was needed per 80lb lamb. The solution was very strong and could kill if the mixture was too generously given. Frost and Southwick, Chemists and Agricultural Specialists, made up potions for livestock. Stockholm Tar was used to heal cuts and maggot damage. A stream on Little Garway Farm was dammed to make a sheep wash. It ran deep, so when a helper fell in during one sheep-washing season, only his boots could be seen above the surface. Neighbouring farmers used the wash for their sheep too.

Washing the sheep before shearing improved the fleece for the spinners and wool trade. Shearing was done by means of hand shears. However, Gerry Benjamin from Hillside acquired a hand powered shearing machine and took it from farm to farm on his bicycle. Assistants were needed to turn the handle as well as catching the sheep and wrapping the fleece.

Compulsory dipping of sheep had been introduced at the beginning of the century to prevent sheep scab and to kill blowflies. Shepherds were watched by village policemen to see that each sheep endured its proper baptism in chemicals. P.C. Greg was particularly conscientious about hill sheep and if he found one on the hill that had not been dipped he had the power to insist that all the sheep should be redipped. A dip was built in the fold yard well away from any watercourse and local farmers would bring their sheep to the Little Garway dip. By the late 1950s dialdrin was successfully used to kill off parasites on sheep, but it was withdrawn from sale when scientific experiments discovered a risk to human health.

Gerry Benjamin with his hand-powered shearing kit

More hefted flocks were kept on the hill in the 1940s and '50s than now. Wilf Whistance had 120 Welsh ewes running there. It takes a while to train sheep to remain in their own little flock. Wilf's method was to entice his sheep off the hill into a nearby field each night using sheep cake. The sheep were happy to come into the sweeter grass in the field. The sheep from other graziers' flocks were not allowed into the hefting field. Slowly the sheep accepted that they were collected in the adjoining fields and would be easily rounded up for lambing, worming, shearing etc.

Sheep handling in the foldyard

Sheep dipping to prevent scab and blowflies

May with children Rosemary, Patrick and Prudence feeding a tiddler lamb

Wilf stopped putting sheep on the hill when one year some became blind due to eating bracken which had caused vitamin deficiency.

Sheep dogs were valued members of the family. Wilf would insist on his dog following him into the house even if May had just washed the floor. He did breed a few spaniels as gun dogs too. Hoping to train his dog to the gun, Wilf took a spaniel to a fox shoot organised by Mr Watkins at The Corras, Kentchurch. A fox was run to ground and terriers dug it out. However the fox went to run away again, dogs followed and a bystander shot into the dogs in an attempt to kill the fox. Wilf's spaniel was shot and injured. Wilf was very annoyed and Patrick had to carry the poor dog, all the way home, cradled in his arms.

The Milk Marketing Board was formed in 1932. It had government backing, as there was a need to provide cities with fresh milk. Free milk was supplied to schools from 1934. Several farms on the hill produced milk. Stony Farm, Oldfield, Cherry Orchard, Hawthorn Well, White Rocks Farm, New Buildings (now Tanglewood) all had churns to be collected by the milk lorry everyday. Eddie Smith at Belleview and Lower Castree had a Jersey herd and all of his milk was used to make butter. George Blake from Little Castlefield kept no cows but delivered milk around the White Rocks houses. The cows were milked by hand and the milk needed to be cooled before being poured into the churns. At Little Garway, Wilf's children were expected to help milk the cows and Rosemary and Patrick became adept at hand milking before and after school. Jenny got an enormous kick in the face from one reluctant milker. Little Garway had a milking machine installed in 1953. To comply with standards for milk production the duck pond was filled in to prevent the cows drinking there. At this time the calves were being sold at market at a fortnight old. In the early '60s compulsory TB testing of cattle was introduced.

At Oldfield Jack did not start milking until 1959. His herd grew to 40 cows but as he had insufficient water on the farm he did not expand

Wilf and Trix, his spaniel

when bulk tanks were introduced in 1964. During the winter of 1963 the roads were blocked solid for several weeks. The milk lorry could not get up the hill so Garway Hill farmers took their churns across the fields to Wormelow.

Livestock need bedding to keep their winter housing clean and for this Garway Hill common provided bracken which was cut and baled. Pat Whistance remembers baling 600 bales of bracken in the 1950s. It needed to be harvested well, allowed to wilt and then dry out. The hard stalks made it very difficult to handle. One year in the '50s, helpers clearing the bracken decided to burn a patch that was too difficult to cut, but soon the fire was out of control. Other graziers were angry that their grass had been burnt as well as the bracken. One year when bracken cutting and collecting coincided with capital works being done by Arthur Barrell, trouble emerged. The tractor pulling a trailer of loose bracken tied down with ropes, caught a post and pulled down the entire wall that Arthur had just completed. Pat stopped baling the fern when one year all his efforts were wasted as having baled up 500 bales of bracken and before he could return with a trailer, all the strings on the bales had been cut and the bales were lost.

Poultry and pigs were invaluable on farms throughout the decades. Most farms and smallholdings would have a pig and a few chickens. Pigs were killed to help feed the family throughout the winter. Trotman Smith would come from Orcop to kill the pig. Hams were salted and hung up in the kitchen and bacon cut on demand, whilst brawn was made from the pig's head. Faggots and sausages were another delicacy. The fat was rendered down to make lard.

It invariably fell to the farmer's wife to keep the chickens. At Little Garway May Whistance's poultry numbers increased from 50 in 1943 to 200 in 1955. They were all free-range hens living in hen houses about the fields. Eggs were collected daily from the poultry huts in the fields and dirty ones wiped clean, then stacked in trays of 30 and piled six deep into wooden double crates ready for collection. The West Midland egg packers from Holmer Road in Hereford came to the farm once a week to collect them.

Geese and turkeys were reared for the Christmas market and the Whistance family's Christmas preparations were put on hold until the last bird had been dressed, usually on Christmas Eve. Young turkey chicks were bought in and reared in a special brooder. Geese would hatch goslings themselves and were very protective of their brood. When the time came for the birds to be killed, Wilf would dispatch them with a knife to the throat and the children were expected to hang on to the creature in its last moments. Mrs Powell from Grosmont would come to help dress the poultry. The birds would be feathered in the washhouse by May, with Margaret and helpers all sitting around a big tin bath into which the plucked feathers fell. The dressing was performed in the kitchen and the last remaining tufts of feathers burnt off over a small methylated spirits stove. One day Mrs Powell unfortunately tipped the small stove over and highly inflammable methylated spirits poured down her leg, resulting in a painful burn and a stay in hospital.

One year Pat's baby ferrets got out and killed all the baby goslings, so no Christmas geese feathering that year. Another year the girls had a favourite pet, a Chinese goose called Gulliver, which May considered would make an excellent Christmas roast for someone. Fortunately the school bus came back earlier than usual that fateful day and

Gulliver was spared thanks to the girls' pleas for a stay of execution which were obviously so persuasive that Gulliver was allowed to die of old age.

During the war several Garway Hill families opened their homes to evacuees. One such child, Sheila Orr, arrived at Little Garway Farm aged 18 months, wearing a white dress in which she was reluctant to walk and run about. May soon made more robust clothing for her to wear and

Dick in the shafts pulling a cart with Rosemary, Patrick and Sheila (evacuee) on board

Sheila became part of the family, staying with the family, or with May's mother in Orcop, until she was 8. If she had stayed at home in East London she may well have been killed, for during an air raid a bomb went flying through her bedroom window. Other evacuees included Mrs Pymer from Welwyn Garden City.

Diversification was a key word in the Whistance household at Little Garway. The farmhouse has six bedrooms and is south facing with a glorious view of the Monnow valley and the hills beyond. It proved to be a popular place for holidays and May, who advertised farm holidays in a London newspaper, soon had visitors arriving for a week's full board. Satisfied 'paying guests', as May called them, often repeated these holidays. Patrick can remember the Clark family from London coming for several years running. He most remembers that Mr Clark was a schoolmaster with a rather stern manner. Major Symonds, Miss Cusons and Mrs Parker are also remembered. The holidaymakers placed orders for Christmas poultry and so May dispatched dressed geese by train to London and other destinations.

From 1939 until 1952 Margaret Watkins helped May inside the farmhouse and also with outside duties. Now in her 80s Margaret can remember helping to catch and prepare rabbits for a hearty stew and churning the buttermilk until it changed to butter. She remembers walking with Pat, carrying the wireless battery accumulator, through deep snow in the winter of 1947, to have it charged at Northgate House by Mr Wergen. Margaret married Albert Benjamin in 1952 and moved to Hillside Farm, Garway Hill.

In 1938, Ross District Council bought rights to water on Little Garway farm, built a reservoir and piped water to stand pipes down in the village of Garway. The supply continued to be used until the late 1990s but was supplemented by supplies from a spring on the Kesty brook at Trevannon. Mains electricity arrived on the hill in 1961. Mains water became available once the reservoir was built by the Rock Mount road in the 1970s.

In the 1950s government grants were made available to build barns, and Wilf had two Dutch barns and two cattle sheds built. As the decades passed fewer workers were employed on the farm. Tony Smith regrettably left to work in Hereford. Patrick and later Jennifer joined by Arthur, Wilf's nephew from Cardiff, worked together on the farm. Daughters Jenny and Prudence decided to work in Australia for two years and Patrick began to run the farm alone, with seasonal help at lambing time and contractors for hedging and combining. He began keeping Essex Saddleback sows and crossing them with a Large White Boar, letting them run in Oldfield wood and Devils Cave. The butcher considered the carcasses too fat and so he changed over to keeping Welsh lop sows together with the Large White boar. He built a farrowing house and a fattening house and through the late 1970s and '80s he could house 300 pigs at any one time. In 1988 the last pigs left Little Garway as prices fluctuated so much that the project was no longer viable.

In 1965 Hereford Council, following a government initiative, asked all commoners to register their common rights. Disputes about the number of sheep each commoner was allowed led to a legal battle in 1973.

Foot and Mouth was found in the Corras sheep in April 2001, meaning that all the livestock on and surrounding Garway Hill Common had to be slaughtered. On Easter

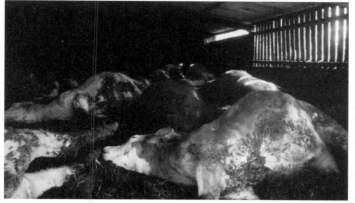

Monday 16 April 2001 at Little Garway Farm, 33 Hereford Friesian Cross suckler cows, their baby calves and 60 fattening cattle, one Charolais bull, 450 Suffolk cross ewes and their lambs, 50 ewe lambs and 10 Suffolk rams were slaughtered. When the livestock had been collected in and handed over to the slaughtermen, Patrick drew the curtains in the sitting room, sat down on the settee and sobbed. It seemed that all those years of work and effort had been brought to a sudden, unnecessary and painfully sad end. Looking at the piles of dead carcasses the following day was even more heartbreaking. For many days afterwards, smoke from funeral pyres could be seen and smelt all round the hill. Large tipper

Culled livestock due to Foot and Mouth, Easter Monday, 16 April 2001

lorries carried dead stock that was not burnt to a tip near Pershore. Soon the hill had no livestock at all except Jack Heath's at Oldfield and Mike Sparey's from Demesne. But they inevitably suffered problems looking after their stock's welfare, as they were unable to move animals across roads to fresh fields or to sell any of them. Clean up gangs then came to work on the hill farms. Disinfectant points washed vehicle wheels from 8.00am until 4.30pm when the gangs went home.

Eventually, everyday life returned to normal and stocking rates on hill farms were back to previous levels by September 2002. During the time when no sheep or ponies were kept on the hill the bracken became more invasive than ever. By June 2004 Liz Cornwell and Lesley Whistance remarked that something had to be done. In December 2004 the Garway Hill Commoners Association was formed with the intention of reducing the amount of bracken on the hill.

Looking back over the 20th century it is clear that as the years rolled by people left the farms to find their fortunes elsewhere. More animals were farmed with fewer herdsmen to tend them as mechanisation and intensive methods increased. Successive governments sought cheap food and lots of it, giving subsidies to assist in this objective. Now as the 21st century unfolds, the government is encouraging farmers to keep fewer animals and to farm for wildlife with permanent pastures restored. Huge quantities of food are being sourced from abroad. Unfortunately, supermarkets have a stranglehold over farm prices. There are now only 45 dairy farms in the whole of Herefordshire, with none being on Garway Hill. Peter Morris, who lives at Belle Vue on Garway Hill, has kept his old diaries and that for April 1987 records 17kilo dead weight lambs selling for £51.50 in Hereford Market auctions. Twenty years later, in April 2007, the same weight lambs made £45 in Hereford market. What does the future hold?

The average age of a Garway Hill farmer is 60. He may moan and shake his head about the latest EU directive but when all is said and done there can be no better working and living environment than farming on Garway Hill.

Little Garway in 1999

9 'Bread & Beer'

Garway Hill pre-1900

Prior to the Orcop Enclosure Award of 1820 the common, which was open land covered with bracken and scrub, stretched down as far as the bottom lane on the eastern side and in some cases below this. Being common land few if any people would have been living on it, although there is evidence that there was insidious encroachment for agricultural purposes. It therefore follows that there was little or no demand for services or retail outlets in the area and this would have been the case until the new owners of the enclosures developed their land for agriculture.

Once the land had been divided up and the plots became individually owned, some of the owners began building cottages for themselves and their families on their land. Today many of these houses still have an attached field which is possibly a leftover from the Enclosure Awards. In the main the houses were simple cottages, comprising of two living rooms on the ground floor and two bedrooms above. There were of course no mains services, water being obtained from the few properties that had wells or from springs. Some rights to obtain water from these wells still exist, though unlikely to be used nowadays. However, I know several families that still use natural spring water off the hill although they also have the back up of being connected to the mains.

The whole family of parents and several children lived in these small houses and, not uncommonly, some extended family members as well. Conditions had therefore to be very cramped. It was unusual that a house would have a name and was likely to be referred to as 'a cottage' or just 'on Garway Hill'. It is therefore very difficult to connect the known families who were living in the area, from census data, with specific houses.

The census records do, however, show that many adults had two or more jobs, not only looking after their own house, family and land but also having specific trades such as mason, chimney sweep, house keeper, blacksmith, dairymaid, cook, post mistress, inn keeper, dressmaker, sawyer, shoemaker and shopkeeper. It was not unusual for the men to also hire themselves out as agricultural or general labourers. There were also, of course, the farmers.

Garway Hill post-1900

Much of the detail below was acquired from people who have lived in the area for most if not all of their lives, with either first hand knowledge, or what they have learned over the years from family or acquaintances.

Shops, pubs and services found on and around Garway Hill

The hamlet of Bagwyllydiart is situated in the north-west corner of Orcop parish and therefore north of Garway Hill on a cross-roads at which the four parishes of Orcop, Kilpeck, Kentchurch and Garway meet. The road which runs east/west is a well used route connecting the A465 Abergavenny/ Hereford road at Pontrilas to the main A49 which is the major north/south road connecting Bristol through Ross-on-Wye to Hereford and beyond to Shrewsbury.

The New Inn at Bagwyllydiart in the early 1960s, now called Bagwyllydiart House and, below, as it is today

The New Inn, although long closed, stands at the crossroads. In 1867 it was occupied by William Meadmore, one of the many Meadmores who lived (and still do so) in the area. James Smith and his wife, Jane Smith, and their two children were at the inn in 1876. By 1905 the Alton Court Brewery owned the New Inn and James Norris was the landlord. The pub sold not only the usual beer, wine and spirits, but also cigarettes and sweets etc. much as a modern pub does today. Also it had pumps outside selling petrol which were hand operated.

*Coles shop photographed in about 1890. (*Hereford Times *staff photo Ray Lloyd)*

A detail from the Scudamore Papers indicating the presence of a coffee house at The Stone Wall. (HRO 830 c.1730)

The sale of petrol continued after the pub closed in 1962 but ceased some years ago. Lilla Smith who ran the pub with her husband, Tom, remembers that the cottage next door was at one time a pub called The Squirrel. Apparently The Squirrel was thought to be inadequate by the brewery and they built a new pub next door calling it The New Inn, and the Squirrel ceased to trade.

If one travels south from the Bagwyllydiart crossroads, signposted to Garway Hill, and bear left at the Garway Methodist chapel to pass High House Farm on your right you can see a house up on the right bank called Old Orchard, which was at one time a grocers shop. Ernie and Edith Adamson bought Old Orchard in May 1920 and they set up this shop which they ran until the summer of 1948. Apart from grocery items they also sold paraffin. Many of the items for sale were bought wholesale from Coles of Pontrilas. Locals called it the 'Bottom Shop' because it was on the bottom road.

Then carry on further down the road and turn up the first lane on the right. This is Baker's Lane and the house now called Birch Banks, 150 yards along on the right, (which was originally called Tulip Cottage, then Tudor Cottage) was where the Badham family sold flour. Also on the lane, but demolished some years ago, was a small house where a cobbler called Baker lived. His father owned land on both sides of the lane hence, it is thought, the name Baker's Lane. It is quite unusual for roads and lanes to have names in this area.

Turn left at the top of Baker's Lane and as you travel along the road the field to your right slopes up hill. There is a green lane here that runs along the top edge of the field called Camdore lane, although it has been called Snow Lane. At one time in the 17th century there was a house called The Stone Wall and this was a most likely site for a Coffee House. Above is a detail from Scudamore Papers — this being the only written proof found of its existence.

Further on along the road, the next house on the right is Glendower, where there was an upstairs ballroom which was used within living memory.

Continuing on along this road you come to Malvern View. This, until 1972, was also a shop. Many of

Glendower today

The Top Shop 1972 — just before the Arthur family gave up their business

these 'shops' really were just family houses in which one room or an outhouse served as the shop. Malvern View, however, was a general provision shop properly fitted out with counter and shelves and was locally called the 'Top Shop' on account of being on the top road.

Twice a week the local doctor held a surgery there. This was held in one of the front rooms, so as you entered the house you turned left for the shop or right for the surgery. This room was actually the Arthur family's living room. The buildings to the left of the house were where the animal feeds and other agricultural goods for sale were stored.

Just around the corner from Malvern View on the left hand side is Cherry Orchard Farm, at one time a cider house which later became the local abattoir selling fresh meat.

There was also a carrier called White who at one stage worked out from Cherry Orchard. It is now solely a farm.

Further down the road on the right is Dingle Cottage. This was a Post Office from the turn of the century until the early 1930s when the Post Office moved to the house across the road from Sun Farm — originally The Rising Sun public house.

Post Offices were very important to rural communities as letters and telegrams were

Dingle Cottage which was the Post Office until the mid 1930s

The Globe pub before the Second World War (left) and (right) present owner Tony Smith and his brother Tom as young men outside the Globe where they grew up. Tom was to marry Lilla Meadmore and they ran the New Inn at Bagwyllydiart until that also closed

the only practical means of communicating over a long distance. You also could buy postal orders which were the forerunners of cheques. These in their turn are rapidly being outdated. Many people in rural areas did not have the advantage of being able to go to banks and therefore did not have bank accounts other than money held in the Post Office.

The Globe is 200yds further along the road and was run as a pub for almost 100 years, between 1867 and 1957. Tobacco and cigarettes were sold here together with beer and cider but it did not double up as a shop. The present owner of The Globe was, as a child, living at the pub when his parents ran it.

Travelling on down the road one comes to Sun Farm on the left and across the road is a house called The Sun. Originally this was called The Rising Sun and was a pub, though now always referred to as The Sun. The Sun Lane, running beside the building, leads up to the common. The Rising Sun was a small beer house which operated roughly between 1870 and 1920. It was owned by Watkins Brewery of Hereford and later the Tredegar Brewery. As a pub it was probably never

Opposite Sun Farm, this was formerly The Rising Sun pub

very successful. It did, however, have a small first-floor ballroom where local people can remember going to dances.

During the '30s the Post Office was moved from The Dingle to the Sun and was run by a Mrs Howells. Her husband, Jim, a bus driver, worked for a garage in Hereford. Jim used to make the last bus journey to Garway Hill each day and kept the bus at what is now called Bedlam Cottage overnight, making the return trip to Hereford, picking up passengers, first thing in the morning.

After Mrs Howells, a Mrs Burrows ran the shop before it was taken over by the Gardiners in 1937 from when it was run by Mrs Gardiner until 1973. Initially it was just run as a post office but in the 1940s this was expanded to provide some groceries. It also became a sub-library and once a fortnight a library van came and changed the books which were kept in a box. They also had the only phone in the area — number 15 — on which locals could make calls. Mrs Gardiner's husband, Herbert, worked on a farm, but also ran a small haulage business a main part of which was buying and selling coal which he got from South Wales.

In 1973 the house was sold to Mansy Fay of Upper Moors Farm who in turn rented it out to a group of hippies. Locally it is said Mansy Fay thought himself 'King of the Hippies'. They ran a wholefood shop for about a year and then drifted away.

After the hippies left there were no further business activities and the house once again became a domestic dwelling.

Attached to the former pub, this was the post office and then the shop which closed in the mid 1970s. The sign of the shop is on the wall of the building. This had no association with The Rising Sun pub apart from its name. It is now very well known and used widely as a route marker

The garage for Les Gardiner's bus (as seen today), which he built for that purpose

Les Gardiner, Herbert's son, ran a bus business from the early '50s until the late '80s. Apart from private bookings he transported the children of the area to and from Ross Grammar School until that in turn closed and became John Kyrle High School.

'Bronco' Bill Sayce of High House Farm also ran a bus with which he transported children to and from school in Hereford.

At one time there was a corn merchant at Garrondale and there was a mill on the Garron brook further down the hill.

From the Sun, if one heads towards Garway, the next turning on the right leads to White Rocks which is a hamlet on the southern side of Garway Hill. It is rather remote and one would think likely to be self-contained. Surprisingly I have come across no evidence of any shop or pub. In fact, I understand that in days gone by the people of White Rocks walked over the hill and used the pubs and shops in Orcop parish. The only mention of any form of service to the public was that there was at one time a Sunday School at Chantry Cottage. From the name one can only assume that the site has past religious significance.

Further along the southern edge of the common was a farm called Hill Farm. The late Mrs Annie Ward of Little Castlefield farm recalled that about 50 to 60 years ago this building was a ruin with no roof, but had a large carved stone over the mantelpiece. When Garway was part of the Monmouthshire Poor Law Union this building was used as a 'workhouse' and the inmates worked the farm. The building has now disappeared — stone is so readily recyclable.

On the west side of the hill lies the parish and village of Kentchurch which once had two pubs, one of which is still in business. The Bridge Inn has been open from the mid-19th century to the present day. This is an area much associated with the exploits of the legendary Jack O'Kent and one of the stories is depicted on the pub sign (see

The Bridge Inn which is still a popular one

also p.144). Near The Bridge Inn there was a Post Office which is now a private residence.

The other pub was The Royal Oak which existed from the 1870s until the First World War when it closed. The house that was once this pub is situated on the road leading uphill from Pontrilas towards Orcop. The hill is about half a mile long and is called Spite House Hill; the house of this name is long gone but the name remains. Continue along this road and you come to Bagwyllydiart where we first started.

The Bridge Inn sign of Jack of Kent and the Devil

Before the First World War the area around Garway Hill was fairly remote with poor roads, particularly in autumn and winter. All of the roads leading to and around the hill had steep climbs that were taxing to travellers but especially those involved in the carrying of goods and freight. That just mentioned, Spite House Hill up from Pontrilas, would have challenged horse drawn vehicles leaving for Orcop and still proves daunting to modern vehicles in bad weather even today. In severe winters local farmers are sometimes asked to tow them to the top.

The old Post Office at Kentchurch as it is now

In the early 1900s the movement of freight was principally by horse drawn carts and wagons, but as the means of transport developed carriers used lorries which allowed for larger loads and shorter journey times. There were several carriers

The Royal Oak as it is today

around the area who would transport almost anything around the district. Nowadays they are called Transport Companies or Logistics firms. Some of the carriers also started to take passengers on a regular basis to Hereford and Ross, even to the extent of providing timetables and pick up and drop off points — in reality an early bus service.

The Industrial Revolution brought about a significant increase in the wealth of British people, eventually leading to greatly improved living standards for those in remote agricultural areas such as Garway Hill. This in turn created opportunities for traders eagerly looking for new areas of business. The opening up of this whole area began with the building of the railway, together with the station at Pontrilas in 1853.

The later improvements in road transport paved the way for the traders with their delivery vans, who provided a valuable service to country areas before the proliferation of the motor car which changed everything. In those early days many now long forgotten traders sold their wares to those on 'The Hill'. However, some of the names are still remembered and deserve to be recorded for posterity. All of these small retail and service outlets were very important to the convenience and character of the local rural communities.

In addition to Coles of Pontrilas, previously mentioned, there was Mr Leslie Drayson Russell who delivered to Garway Hill from his large grocery and bakery shop in Hoarwithy from 1920 until he retired when the war ended in 1945. In the period between the wars a bakery known as Timmings and Godding of Pontrilas were delivering bread to this area. In the late 1940s Edwin Davies of King's Caple and later on of Brockhampton, started a delivery service with a Ford 8 car, later replaced by a large box van that carried a very extensive range of household goods. With the arrival of the first supermarkets in the mid 1960s, this rather astute grocer closed his business and became manager of one such supermarket in Ross-on-Wye.

Between the years of 1956 and 1972, when he retired and closed his grocery shop in Hoarwithy, Mr Jack Topping served the area. Badgers of Wormelow were also trading locally during the 1970s up until the early 1980s. Burtons, a Hereford grocer, delivered to the area as did Kears, who were a large bakery business, also from Hereford. Gurneys of Hereford were delivering pre-ordered groceries and in the late 1960s, Ernie Florence with his large mobile shop served the area.

Of the butchers, Mailes of Ewyas Harold are the longest survivors having delivered to Garway Hill for generations and still do so today. From the late 1930s up until the late 1950s there was also Harry Gundy who had butchers shops at Llanwarne and Hoarwithy. There was also Babbage and Hamlyn of Broad Street, Ross-on-Wye making deliveries in the 1940s and '50s. Their delivery driver was a Mr Frost. Later there was H.A. Rutherford of St Martins Street, Hereford. Ross Laundry, a very substantial business, provided a regular laundry service until it closed in about 1980.

Before the war, Bert Gardiner was the local coal delivery man. In recent years coal deliveries have been by Mr Bill Hoare from the Forest of Dean who was replaced by Mr Parker, also from the Forest.

The local Police Station was at St Weonards with the Magistrates' Court at Harewood End. Both have now closed and Garway Hill is policed from Peterchurch.

With the coming of the railway in 1853 Pontrilas rapidly grew into a very busy village. There was a cattle market, visiting banks, shops and a range of light industry. Coles' shop developed in importance, both retail and wholesale, and sold a wide range of products including groceries, clothing and hardware items. They ran a delivery service to a wide area including Orcop, White Rocks and Garway Hill. The closure of the Golden Valley Railway, for passenger traffic in 1941 and goods in 1948, was indicative of the changes destined to affect this busy place. Some years later, in 1958, the main line station of Pontrilas was also to close which added to the isolation and rapid decline of the village. Increasing prosperity leading to mass ownership of private cars and widespread use of trucks, lorries and vans, meant that most of these local services were no longer viable. John Cole of Coles shop in Pontrilas wrote in the *Hereford Times*: 'Village shops are dying out with the arrival of big supermarkets and it is becoming increasingly difficult to keep my sort of business alive'.

Certainly the shops and pubs have virtually all closed but there are still specialist services centred on the area, such as physiotherapy, chiropody, cranial massage, computer support, an architect, a builder, carpenter and joiner as well as telephone and computer based businesses. There are still a number of transport firms but their trade is of an industrial nature, not just serving individual needs as in the past. But now with the rapid development of information technology, locally based businesses are again on the increase.

10   The Garway Bus

One of the earliest records of Garway people being taken to town must surely be that of Mrs Ellen Nicholls, antecedent of the Nicholls families of this parish. Back in the early 1900s this intrepid woman would use her pony and trap to carry fare-paying passengers to and from Monmouth. Such carriers with their horse-drawn vehicles were forerunners of the bus services that were destined to put them out of business. The Kelly's *Directory* for 1914 indicates that there were three carriers working out of Garway with George Nicholls going to the Angel Inn, Monmouth on Fridays; Jane Webb to the Kings Head, Ross-on-Wye on Thursdays; and Amos Barrell to The Plough, Hereford on Wednesdays and Saturdays. George Nicholls was listed as a cottage farmer which tends to indicate that being a carrier was but a sideline. By 1922 they had all gone.

Although the first bus in Hereford made its appearance during July 1908, it was not until 1924 that the inhabitants of Garway Hill were to receive the benefits of similar public transport. In 1919 the bus services nationwide began to rapidly expand and this was to have a profound effect on the lives of the masses as many of the remote rural areas did not have easy access to the railway network which was in any event a luxury which they could not afford. Even if these people had been able to afford bicycles, the rough roads of that period would have made them unsuitable for long journeys. The bus provided new opportunities, overcoming the physical barriers that had for so long impeded social movement. Ultimately this would lead to increased employment and indeed marriage prospects, as people became able to escape from the constraints of isolation.

During the early years of bus transport the bureaucratic barriers that had to be overcome greatly impeded its development. Hundreds of local authorities were responsible for issuing operating licences, often displaying a parochial and xenophobic attitude to outsiders. This continued until the Road Traffic Act of 1930 transferred these powers to thirteen Regional Traffic Commissioners.

Following the end of the Great War large numbers of lorries were being disposed of by the War Department, being considered surplus to requirements after the 'war to end all wars'. Many were purchased by returning servicemen displaying entrepreneurial talents and aided by their small demobilisation gratuities. Considerable numbers of these lorries were converted into buses.

In 1924 Mrs L.G. Capper of Northgate, St Weonards was to take her first tentative steps into the competitive world of public transport. She was the wife of Captain Capper whose family were considered to be minor country gentry. They farmed at Northgate from where they also ran a contract threshing business. Mrs Capper was a woman of Swiss descent who obviously had business aspirations and probably raised a few eyebrows when she ventured into the world of 'trade', which was still regarded with an element of disdain amongst the gentry.

It was a bold and somewhat risky venture by Mrs Capper, as in the same parish was a Mr E.W. Howell who had set up his own bus service some four years earlier. Fortunately for Mrs Capper, this service to Hereford via Orcop did not pass over Garway Hill. Mrs Capper's first bus was actually a Ford model T lorry fitted out with movable bench seats and open to the elements. During its first Wednesday of service there was apparently a snowfall that must have made it a miserable journey. Soon afterwards, much to the relief of passengers no doubt, a steel frame was fitted covered with a heavy canvas cover. The first route covered by the Northgate bus was to Hereford via Garway Hill and Orcop following the same route as the present day service. It was quite normal for these sort of services to be on market days only and, being run by a farming family, it was not unusual for passengers to share their space with a couple of weaner pigs on their way to market. Just as today, the road followed a very winding route around the hill that was yet to be covered with a tarmac surface, making for a rough journey. But as any countryman would have told you, 'a second class ride is better than a first class walk'.

A service to Pontrilas was introduced, probably with the aim of connecting with the Hereford to Abergavenny railway together with its branch line through the Golden Valley to Hay-on-Wye. This may not have been financially viable for it was soon discontinued.

In these early days bus services tended to be restricted to market days. Initially, Mrs Capper did not run a Saturday bus service to Hereford on account of her two buses being used to go to Ross and Abergavenny. One has to remember that country areas were at that time very self-sufficient and the need to travel to the towns was not great; very few people would have lived in the countryside with their workplace being in the town. It was not until the Education Act of 1944 that country children began to travel to the towns and city schools for their secondary education. This was the period before the increasing industrialisation of the market town of Hereford and also before the farms became highly mechanised leading to large-scale loss of jobs in agriculture.

During her years in business, Mrs Capper was to own a total of five different passenger vehicles, starting with the Ford lorry conversion and followed by a Crossley. Then came a GMC T16 single deck bus saloon of 19 seats with a front entrance. The registration number was CJ 8028 and was first registered

The third bus purchased by Mrs L.G. Capper for her Northgate fleet was this GMC T16 19-seater, registration number CJ 8028, registered in June 1925. (John Howell)

in 1925. A Lancia bus saloon with 27 seats came next with registration number CJ 8667 and was first registered in 1926. Finally came a Dennis single deck bus saloon of 20 seats with a registration number VJ 1252 and was first registered in 1928. Fixed to the back of her coaches was a vertical ladder, which enabled the driver to stack the market goers' large shopping baskets and boxes on the roof.

What was obviously a more profitable service than the Pontrilas run, was that across country starting at St Weonards and heading through Hoarwithy, across the river to King's Caple, turning towards Brockhampton, thence on through Fownhope and Mordiford and finally to its destination, Hereford. Once again, it was just a Wednesday market day service.

The other service routes catered for by the Northgate bus ran from St Weonards to Abergavenny via Grosmont, with other routes being St Weonards to Monmouth and St Weonards to Ross-on-Wye. These were all on respective market days. To avoid competition with the more powerful bus operators, Mrs Capper concentrated on the indirect routes untapped by her bigger rivals. Where direct competition occurred she would also undercut her local competitor, Mr Howell, who in turn was obliged to lower his fares which was a recipe for disaster, as it would have reduced their profit margins.

In the present day amongst the ever-increasing regulations, it is hard to imagine the incredible overcrowding that took place on these early buses. Apparently, although the Capper bus only had seats for 19 passengers, on Saturday nights as many as 45 would cram on board. On the steepest hills the sheer weight would have been beyond the capacity of this struggling little petrol engine and surplus passengers would be expected to disembark

By the Royal Hotel, Ross-on-Wye, is this 1927 Albion PM28,
registration number CJ 9898, a 32-seater belonging to Hereford Transport Ltd.
(Brian Thomas Collection)

and walk to the top of the rise. What stoic uncomplaining people country folk were in those days!

The other St Weonards bus owner, Mr Evan William Howell, was a rather 'well to do' farmer of Church Farm, a County Councillor and a Justice of the Peace. His first involvement with transport came in 1920 when he formed a partnership with James Fryer Ltd of Hereford. Their first bus was an ex-War Department AEC lorry converted to a bus by a Hereford coachbuilder and was registered on 27 February 1920. It was garaged at Church Farm and the driver was Mr Sam Williams, chauffeur to Mr Howell. This was soon followed by a second AEC bus which was based at Newtown, some eight miles north-east of Hereford. Their buses were affectionately known as 'the little yellow buses'. Two months after opening this partnership, a company, to be called Hereford Transport Ltd, was registered with an authorised capital of £20.000. Mr Howell was a Director with Colonel Thomas Wilks appointed Managing Director, the latter having become a Director of Fryers in 1919. Very soon they were joined on the board by Colonel Frank Searle, an eminent motor engineer. Both of these men had served in the Tank Corps during the Great War and before that they had been employed by the Daimler Motor Company. The Fryer business was absorbed by this new company.

Mr Howell appears to have been a shrewd businessman and became the largest individual shareholder. The Hereford Transport Company was a rather grand, possibly pretentious, name for a little company still in its infancy but destined for considerable growth.

By 1922 the St Weonards based bus was operating a service to Abergavenny on Tuesdays; to Hereford on Wednesdays and Saturdays; to Ross on Thursdays and to Monmouth on Fridays and alternate Mondays. With garages at St Weonards, St Owen Street in Hereford and at Newtown, the buses were strategically placed to reduce wasted mileage. The land and garage in St Owen Street was on a three-year lease with an annual rent of £50 to £55. By 1924 there appeared to have been five shareholders in addition to Mr Howell, whose ultimate aim was to have complete ownership of the company.

One of the two Daimler saloon buses owned by Hereford Transport Ltd. was this 1920 model, a 26-seater fitted with a Jennings body. It was photographed near to Mr Howell's Church Farm, St Weonards, where it was garaged. The route display board in the window reads: Skenfrith – Llanvetherine – St Weonards which is out of sequence for the Ross-on-Wye to Abergavenny route. (John Howell)

Consequently, on 16 June 1924, an agreement was drawn up between Thomas Wilks, Jane Wilks, John Wilks, George Butcher and Jason Drew who were the shareholders, and Mr E.W. Howell whereby Hereford Transport passed into the sole ownership of Mr Howell. Colonel Frank Searle's name appears on the agreement but not his signature so perhaps he had already left the company. The registered office was at number 3 Arundel Street, Strand, London WC2, and the agreed share value being 14s 2½d. The legal work was done by Mr T.A. Matthews, a Hereford solicitor, at a cost of £31 10 shillings. Mr Howell now became the Managing Director, appointing his wife and son as co-directors.

On 1 July 1926 the Company was licensed by Abergavenny Town Council to run ten buses within a specified distance of the town but only nine appear to have been registered. On the same day company licenses were issued for eight drivers and seven conductors:

Drivers	**Conductors**
William Scott Holt of Michaelchurch	Reginald Turber of Monmouth
Reg. Andrew Vickery of St Weonards	George Stevens of Monmouth
Ernest Tabb of St Weonards	Horace Nicholls of Garway
Stanley Mahoney of St Weonards	Ernest Jenkins of Vowchurch
Edwin Charles Morgan of Monmouth	Trevor Barrel of Garway
Edward Dallow of Monmouth	Baldwin Ruck of Garway
Walter G.E. Smith of Monmouth	Albert John Hince of Weston Beggard
Ernest D. Bowen of Hereford	

The number of buses that they had on the road at any one time was not great but this successful little company attracted the attention of two big operators. Between June and August of 1925 negotiations took place with the Midland Bus Company who then decided not to proceed with the purchase. The legal costs to Mr Howell were £7 19s 9d with an additional charge of £1 for two journeys to St Weonards by Mr T.A. Matthews.

Another approach, this time by Mr John Watts of Red and White Services was to meet with Mr Howell's approval and resulted in the takeover of Hereford Transport Ltd by one

A general licence and driver's licence issued to Hereford Transport Company by Abergavenny Town Council in 1926

of his subsidiary companies, Griffin Services. Initially, Mr Watts disagreed with Mr Howell's valuation and in a letter of 4 August 1926 suggested a revised figure of £5,000. The company name was to survive, albeit under the control of Mr Watts and Mr Bown for the next four years. The end for Hereford Transport Ltd came in 1930 when the various companies within the group were amalgamated with the Red and White Services. This was made feasible due to the passing of the Road Traffic Act of that year.

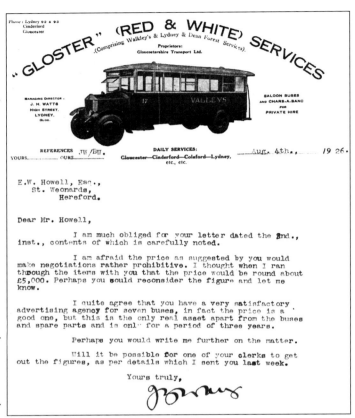

Part of the correspondence in the negotiations for the sale of Hereford Transport Company Ltd to the Red and White Services

Following the sale of his bus company, Mr Howell, who was still living at Church Farm, St Weonards, retired from business at the age of 62. His son, Mr Rhys Howell, sold up at Church Farm in February 1940 but the pioneering spirit continued when his son founded Wye Valley Metals in 1972. In addition to being a Director of this company, at 78 years of age John Howell still runs his 150-acre farm. I was grateful to him for allowing me to copy photographs and documents that have not seen daylight for almost half a century.

For whatever reason, in about 1928 Mrs Capper eventually decided to sell her business which was purchased by her driver, Mr Gwynne Jorden, a farmer's son who lived at Upper Llangunnock on the edge of St Weonards, close to Three Ashes. He was an ambitious man who went on to greatly expand the operation over the next decade. He continued the Garway to Hereford market day service where his eye-catching blue and white buses terminated their journey at St Peter's Square, and from where they departed for the return journey. In 1929 Mr Jorden was operating a somewhat limited weekday service on the route between Ross and Abergavenny. There was also a rather odd arrangement whereby the Red and White ran between Abergavenny and Skenfrith, which is roughly the half-way point, while Jorden's buses completed the section between Skenfrith and Ross-on-Wye. Two years later Mr Jorden had taken over the whole route. By 1932 he was running a comprehensive weekday

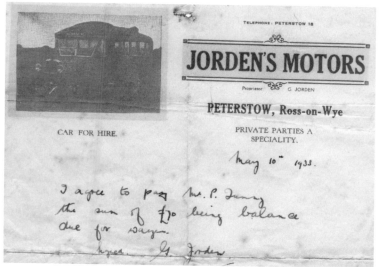

service between the Royal Hotel, Ross-on-Wye and the London Hotel, Abergavenny, passing through Broad Oak every two hours in each direction. The 3.45pm bus from Ross took a detour through Garway. By now Mr Jorden had moved to a more suitable base at The Crofts, Peterstow, which was probably the forerunner of Everstone Garage and which, in turn, is now a small housing estate. In 1937, Mr Jorden's substantial enterprise was taken over by the Red and White Services Ltd.

The origins of the 'Red & White' bus company lay in Tredegar, South Wales, with the formation of 'The Valleys Motor Bus Services' by John Watts of Lydney. He started with three ex-army lorries that were fitted with charabanc bodies. Back home in Lydney, Mr Watts also formed the 'Lydney and Dean Forest Bus Services'. By 1922 he owned a total of 17 buses. In these early days they were plagued with unfair competition from get rich quick merchants who would run a bus just minutes ahead of the scheduled bus. This was a situation that emerged in Herefordshire during the 1980s following de-regulation, a classic case of history repeating itself!

In 1919, another successful business emerged when the 'Griffin Motor Bus Company' was formed at Brynmawr by a Mr Jones and a Mr Bown. 'Valley Motors' quickly became associated with this company and the vision and acumen possessed by these pioneers was to lay the foundations of a great transport business that was to continue to expand for the next 30 years.

In 1930 numerous companies in the group amalgamated as 'Red and White Services' which included 'Griffin Services' who in 1926 had taken over 'Hereford Transport Ltd'. This company served the Hereford, Monmouth, Hay and Michaelchurch area and was perceived to be a link between the South Wales and Forest of Dean theatre of operations. A lengthy article appeared in the *Sunday Express* of 20 November 1932 regarding the phenomenal success of Mr John Watts, stating that the combined group was running 10 million miles a year and carrying 18 million passengers. The whole operation came under the umbrella of 'Red and White United Transport Ltd' in 1937 and was a vast concern. By the time of the nationalisation of all the major passenger traffic companies in 1950, it was the largest independent passenger transport undertaking in the country with its headquarters in Chepstow. On 10 February of that year it passed into public ownership heralding a new dawn for public transport under the control of The British Transport Commission.

One of the most successful local bus companies was 'Wye Valley Motors', generally referred to as 'Morgans' as it was owned by Mr W.E. Morgan who had started his business in 1926 with a converted secondhand lorry garaged on the site of the old chemical works at Pontrilas. One of his first buses was a Reo, registration number DJ1057 that was registered in 1928 and was in

The Wye Valley Motors 32-seater Leyland LT2 bus with registration number VJ 2770 was first registered in May 1930. (Derek Foxton Collection)

service on the Pontrilas – Garway – Hereford route. Both the route and the vehicle were later sold to Mr E.E. Williams of Pontrilas (later of Ewyas Harold) in about 1930. At this time there was an overlap in services with Mr Jorden's buses, particularly between Garway and Hereford over Garway Hill. A reversal took place in 1937 when most of Mr Williams' business was transferred to Mr Morgan which put him back on the Garway Hill route. Mr Morgan expanded his business by gradually taking over other one-man operations and finally taking control of the long established and substantial business of 'Irene Baynham Coaches' of the Swan Garage, Ross-on-Wye in 1963. Wye Valley Motors were eventually to dispose of some of their widespread routes and consolidate their network that covered the south-west area of Herefordshire, including Garway Hill. This was a comprehensive service run at regular intervals, including Sundays which

The home of Wye Valley Motors in St Martins Street, Hereford, as it was in about 1960.
(Derek Foxton Collection)

undoubtedly would have had a much reduced level of service.

During the 1920s High Town was the main bus terminus before it was moved to St Peters Square in 1929. In 1935 a brand new and very large bus station was built by Hereford City Corporation on the site of Hereford Gaol. This was to become the terminus for almost all of the buses entering the city. From 1948, Wye Valley Motors' main storage depot was at Hereford Bus Station between the Gaol Governor's house and the County Hospital with the head office and garage in St Martins Street, Hereford, where a car dealership is now located. A satellite depot was at Market Garage, Pontrilas and this was where the Garway Hill bus was garaged and where in the 1960s the driver, Mr Stanley Mahoney, who had previously driven for Hereford Transport Ltd., was based. During the war he was employed at the Ministry of Supply depot at Pontrilas. His working day included driving a bus belonging to Ford and Reims of Brynmawr to and from that area, collecting workers for the depot.

Prior to the end of the Second World War there was no school bus running to Garway school. Things came to a head on 2 October 1945 when the parents of 28 children who lived on Garway Hill kept them away from school as a protest. The three-mile walk each way to school was indeed unreasonable. This had the desired effect and a school bus was laid on from 8 October. The school hours were altered from 9.30am to a 9am start in the morning and ending at 3.15pm instead of 3.45pm in the afternoon. This was to fit in with the availability of the bus that was probably supplied by Wye Valley Motors. In 1947, due to the heavy snowfalls and continuing hard frosts, the bus was unable to run over Garway Hill for some eight weeks. During the slightly less severe winter of 1963 the bus did not run for five weeks.

In July 1949 the little school at Kentchurch was closed and from 19 September of that year a shooting brake type of vehicle with a timber framed bodywork belonging to Morgans Garage of Ewyas Harold brought the Kentchurch children to Garway School. At a later date Wye Valley Motors took over this service, running a school bus from Pontrilas. Before Orcop School's closure in 1964, Wye Valley Motors were running a bus there from the Kilpeck area.

From the mid 1950s, bus services on a national level were beginning to decline and over the next 20 years passenger traffic was set to decrease by two-thirds. This was due to both social changes and increased operating costs, partly due to fuel tax. Cost cutting was to lead to the introduction of one-man buses but on the Garway Hill route the driver and conductor crews were to continue for some years to come. During this period the company dispensed with the conductor on the early morning and evening bus and a young woman from Garway who worked in Hereford was employed, for a modest wage and free travel, as the conductress. The route followed the very same road as used by the Stage Coach bus company today.

By 1960 the rural bus services were also in decline. The increased prosperity, which was beginning to replace the ongoing austerity of the post war years, brought about a rapid increase in car ownership that enabled country people to take up employment in the towns. By 1970 the Red and White's market day services from Garway to Hereford on Wednesdays and to Monmouth on Fridays were discontinued as was the somewhat sporadic service between Orcop and Ross-on-Wye. Inevitably, during the late 1960s, Wye Valley Motors would have experienced a downturn in their business leading to the usual desperate cost cutting. Mr Morgan died in November 1973 aged 70 and his widow and co-director, sold the whole business to G.H. Yeomans, the large and successful operators from Canon Pyon, who took over with effect from 1 September 1974. Yeomans were then to operate the Garway route until late 1978. By this time the frequency of journeys had been greatly reduced.

In June 1975, a new company was established, owned by Mr Brian Whitehead, a former bus driver from Newent in Gloucestershire, almost 20 miles away from Garway. In late 1978 he took over the Garway to Hereford service from G.H. Yeomans which they had inherited from Wye Valley Motors in 1974. Apparently his nick-name was Flash and so 'Flashes Coaches' came into being. They expanded very rapidly at the expense of quality and

A rare photograph of one of Mr Whitehead's Flashes Coaches taken shortly before the end of an equally rapid rise and fall of an ambitious business venture. This is an ex-Yeomans 1972 Bedford YMQ, registration number WVJ 500K. (Brian Thomas)

by 1983 appear to have been put off the road for this very reason. At a Garway Parish Council meeting around this time fears were expressed over the safety of passengers on the Garway Hill route due to the perceived reckless speeds being reached along narrow roads. Following Prime Minister Margaret Thatcher's disastrous obsession with de-regulation in July 1981 many well-run companies with cash flow problems went out of business. The Transport Act of 1985 was an attempt to sort out the chaos.

Nick Maddy Coaches of Michaelchurch Escley did, for a short while, run a small bus from Broad Oak over Garway Hill to connect with the main road services at Wormelow but this was unprofitable.

It was probably with the withdrawal of Flashes Coaches that Martins coaches of Cross Ash took over. This was a family business owning about ten coaches run by brothers Bill, Jack and sister Jill Martin. Their route to Hereford was rather convoluted starting at Cross Ash, and then heading through Grosmont, Kentchurch, Garway, Bagwyllydiart, Kilpeck, Much Dewchurch, Tram Inn, Cobhall, Allensmore and then to Hereford. This service appears to have continued through the 1980s. They also operated the Garway to Kingstone School run from about 1975 to around 1990. Now in 2007 all of their big coaches have been sold leaving just three or four minibuses on school contracts.

By 1989 First Bus Midland Red had taken over the more direct Garway to Hereford route but still taking in Garway Hill and Orcop. Yeomans, now based in Hereford, were back again in the late 1990s and then came Dukes Coaches from the Forest of Dean in about 2002. Now, in the autumn of 2007, Dukes' entire fleet is to be sold at auction. Each of these bus operators tried their luck on this route with limited success. Service such as this can only continue thanks to a hefty subsidy from Herefordshire Council. After

A Bristol RE belonging to the Red and White photographed in 1980 shortly before the de-regulation of bus services. (Bran Thomas)

a succession of short-lived attempts to fill the gap left by the big companies, the service is once again in safe hands under the umbrella of the huge national concern of Stagecoach, whose services to Garway are unfortunately very limited.

One of the Red and White Company's local routes was from Hereford to Lydney via Monmouth and Coleford, passing close enough to Garway to be accessible. On Thursdays their Abergavenny to Ross bus diverted to Garway to pick up passengers who were going to market. This local service was discontinued in about 1958. During the 1940s and early '50s the 'Red and White' ran a service from Hereford over Orcop and Garway Hill to Monmouth on Fridays, which was of course, market day. Their daily route was from Ross-on-Wye, through Sellack, St Owens Cross, then turning right at the Old Pike for St Weonards. Here it turned around the 'green' and headed back towards Broad Oak and Garway where it would turn at 'Nicholls Turning' by the junction with the Hollow Oak road which leads to Bagwyllydiart, and would then continue its journey to Abergavenny. This was a diversion mainly for the benefit of the Garway schoolchildren that I understand was discontinued in 1972.

Numerous small bus businesses have existed at various times in the area. The dates when they did so, and precisely what they did have been difficult to clarify, so some degree of error is inevitable. They did not run daily services but they certainly fulfilled a social economic need for the local people in what is now seen as a bygone age. During the Second World War there would have been a strong demand for buses to take men and women to work at the vast Royal Ordnance Factory at Rotherwas on the outskirts of Hereford. This must have been a profitable period for William Morgan's Wye Valley Coaches that were covering the route from Garway through Orcop to Rotherwas carrying workers for the three shifts known as the 'Red Shift', the 'White Shift', and the 'Blue Shift'. During and for some years after the war a number of the Wye Valley buses were utility vehicles often referred to as 'Utes' that were fitted out with wooden slatted seats more like those in the 1920s.

There was another wartime bus running over Garway Hill which was an elderly 'Vulcan' belonging to Hereford Motors. The bus, which somehow acquired the nickname of 'the Alma Queen', was for carrying workers to the Ministry of Supply depot at Pontrilas and Abbeydore. This was the storage depot for the Royal Ordnance Factory at Rotherwas and is now used by the army as an SAS training camp.

The bread and butter work of these small bus companies has invariably been conveying children to school. Following on from the closure of most of the small country schools there was a need to collect schoolchildren from a wide catchment area and take them to the remaining village schools such as Garway. As these schools eventually became simply Primary Schools, most of the older children from this area received their secondary education at Kingstone, Ross-on-Wye or Hereford.

Over the years the uses of these buses have been manifold. Annual excursions to the seaside by Church and Chapel Sunday schools together with the bellringers and the choristers was a highlight of the year for so many. Buses to the regular Saturday night dance at village halls such as Ewyas Harold, Sellack, Cross Ash, Little Birch, the Rolls Hall at Monmouth and later Park Hall at Wormelow were often run. The thirst for dancing amongst the Garway and Orcop young people led to the need for two Wye Valley Coaches to be hired for Saturday nights, driven by local drivers Jim Howells and Lionel Gwilliam. Football teams such as Orcop and Broad Oak would have hired a coach to take the team and their supporters to away matches. Schoolchildren would occasionally get a special treat such as an afternoon group visit to the pantomime being performed at the Kemble Theatre in Broad Street, Hereford, in addition to the annual trip to the seaside. Garway and Orcop Women's Institutes would have hired a coach for their social outings. The local public houses such as the Broad Oak Inn, The Garway Moon, The Globe, The New Inn and The Fountain with their darts and skittles teams must have generated welcome extra income for the owner/driver coach operators. Evening trips to the May Fair held in the streets of Hereford were always exciting events. Venturing further afield, Don Nicholls is remembered for his excursion to the 'Great Dorset Steam Fair' in the 1980s. Also on record is a trip from the Garway Moon to London in 1951. Could it have been to the Festival of Britain? There must have been many more now long forgotten events that took place in a more contented time when peoples' expectations were very low in comparison to today.

In the 1950s there were annual outings from the Garway Moon organised by Mrs Strange, the landlady, who would insist on the coach returning by 9.30 pm, obviously mindful of her pub trade. The coaches were Percy Tummey's and the driver was Mr Stan Fryer of Llangarron, where I recently visited him.

Surely the most colourful local bus owner was Mr Bill Sayce who lived at Garway Hill, and was widely known as 'Bronco Bill'. By all accounts he was quite a character, working his small farm and also lorry driving. In 1939 he became the driver of an elderly Vulcan bus owned by Hereford Motor Company which was based in Edgar Street, Hereford. This bus was to ferry workmen from the Garway area to the planned RAF camp at Credenhill that was under construction. This small group was to be part of a gang of men who by April 1940 numbered over 1,000 construction workers. Their next project was at Madley where early in 1941 work began on the construction of the huge aerodrome which was completed in just over six months. In addition to his driving duties, Bronco worked during the day as a sawyer on the site. The Vulcan was garaged at his home.

In 1949, Bill Sayce purchased a second hand Bedford bus which was a 1936 25-seater Duple, from Charlie Bounds of Maylord Street, Hereford and offered it for private hire. Bronco was a man who enjoyed his pint and tales of his exploits abound. Local legend has it that he would drop into the Broad Oak Inn for a 'quick one' while his passengers waited patiently on the bus. Apparently it was not unknown for one of his passengers to drive the bus home from a dance due to him spending the evening in the nearest pub. Nowadays he would attract the attention of the law but attitudes towards drinking and driving were quite different in those days. Carrying seasonal fruit pickers from Hereford to the fruit growing areas of Kingstone and St Owens Cross area were part of his work, as were the travel needs of the local football clubs and various pub teams. In December 1950 Mr Sayce sold his bus and just six years later he died at the age of 50 from a massive heart attack. 'Gone but not forgotten' must surely have been his well-earned epitaph.

The new owner was his brother-in-law, Mr Johnny Williams, who ran his business from Garway Hill for the next decade. He only briefly used Bronco's bus which was 'a bit rough'. Mr Williams, who lived at Well House and later Garway House, purchased a secondhand 29 seater 1947 Bedford Duple, registration number ECJ 892, from Percy Tummey in January 1953. In addition to the bus he also owned a taxi business. His first venture into school transport came when he used a large Humber car that had been given an ash frame conversion by a Hereford coach builder. It was licensed to carry eight passengers and was used to take children who lived at Garway Hill to Ross Grammar School. I well remember seeing it pull up at the school gates on my first day there in 1951. It was an unusual vehicle which I understand was used up until 1954 when the service was taken over by Les Gardiner's green and cream Bedford bus which I believe was still being used some 20 years later. By this time the number of children travelling to this school had increased. The £15 per week for the hire of a bus and driver, paid by the Education Authority in the early 1950s sounds very modest nowadays, but at that time £3 worth of petrol would take a bus to Barry Island and back with a drop to spare. The traditional 'whip around' by satisfied passengers sometimes exceeded the driver's wages for the excursion. Following Les Gardiner's departure I understand that Martins took over this route.

The first recorded journey of Johnny Williams' bus was taking Orcop WI to Pontrilas in January 1952 at a cost of £2. Another example was taking Broad Oak football team to Newcastle near Monmouth, a journey priced at £3. His third bus was a 41-seater Bedford with a Plaxton body. The fourth was another Bedford, this time a 41-seater Duple, registration YEA 820.

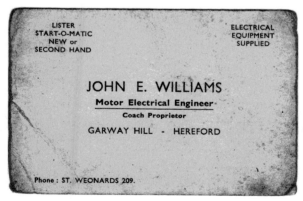

Johnny Williams' business card. (Robin Lamont)

Proudly displaying its owner's name, this 1948 Bedford OB 39-seater was photographed waiting by Well House, Garway Hill, in the early 1950s

A later addition to Mr Williams' fleet was this more modern looking 1958 Bedford Plaxton

Another of Mr Williams' Bedfords was this SB Duple model dating from 1958-59. (Johnny Williams)

In 1957 Mr Williams employed his nephew Bill Sayce who was the son of Bronco Sayce. Bill junior had just completed his National Service in the RAF where he drove buses in Malaya. Part of his duties would now involve picking up members of the Orcop Church congregation on a Sunday from around the scattered parish with a similar service provided for the Women's Institute. Yet another was taking parishioners to the film shows at the parish hall, plus local dances, football matches and pub teams.

Two of Mr Williams' buses were used on the school run to Ross Secondary Modern School with each taking a different route. These pupils were not from the Orcop and Garway area other than those going to the Grammar school, as by this time Kingstone School was providing secondary education for the Orcop and Garway children. In the early 1960s, two of his buses together with the schools contract were sold to Mr Alan Churchill, a former mechanic and driver for Percy Tummey who previously had been a driver for Harry Matthews' Llangrove Transport. The Tummey family were steam engine operators and by the late 1920s Percy had become a bus driver for Jorden's Motors. In January 1934 he bought a half share in Mr H. Matthews' Llangrove Transport and went

Above, a 'special bus' on Mr Jorden's wedding day, c.1932. Percy Tummey is the sixth from the left and Gwynne Jorden is standing alone on the right. This bus is a 1930 Reo FB 20-seater, registration number VJ 2913. The photo on the left is of the same bus at an unknown location, but with 'Garway' as its destination. Percy is on the extreme right. (Joan and Collin Davies)

on to buy out his partner in April 1938. The business became Llangrove Coach Services. In 1961 he sold the business to Baynham's in some sort of partnership deal which brought him financial ruin, and he died on 17 February 1974 aged 73. The remaining Williams' bus was used to take children from Orcop to St Weonards School and from Orcop to Garway. School hours were staggered to accommodate this service. This was following the closure of Orcop School in December 1964 when the remaining pupils were divided between these two schools. Mr Williams also operated two school dinner vans; one working from Hereford delivered to the Golden Valley area whilst the other one delivered from the Ross kitchens. The end came later in the 1960s when with the need for coach hire diminishing and traffic congestion increasing, Mr Williams called it a day.

And so, Johnny Williams' coaches became history, but not so Johnny. Now aged 86 he is still going strong and loves to reminisce. This rather remarkable man deserves a special mention. Together with his Welsh-speaking parents he moved to Garrondale Farm on Garway Hill in 1922. He recalls his first job of driving a water tanker on the construction site of the Ministry of Supply Depot at Pontrilas. On the outbreak of the war he joined the Garway platoon of the Local Defence Force that was soon to be renamed the Home Guard. In 1940, invasion was thought to be imminent and between the hours of 5am and 7am he, together with another lad, would be manning an observation post at the top of Garway Hill, scanning the horizon for German paratroopers who never came. Perhaps they knew that Johnny, armed with his shotgun and single-ball cartridges was waiting for them. In an act of bravado, a member of his platoon shattered a chimney pot of the Globe pub with a single round from his .303 rifle much to the annoyance of the landlord. The culprit's rifle was very soon confiscated on the order of the Company Commander.

This late 1980s line up of coaches belonging to Graham and Don Nicholls was at their yard in Garway. From left to right is a Bedford YRQ, a Leyland Leopard, a Bedford YRQ and another Leyland Leopard. (Graham Nicholls)

Young Mr Williams enlisted in the RAF towards the end of 1940 where he trained as a radar mechanic and for the rest of the war serviced radar sets on Lancaster bombers. Peacetime saw him putting his knowledge of electronics to good use by selling and installing generators in country districts as an agent for Listers of Dursley. He went on to become the owner of The Central Garage of Pontrilas where he tuned racing engines with considerable success.

In about 1954, Les Gardiner became a one-man coach operator specialising in conveying children from the surrounding area to Ross Grammar School, which was eventually to close and amalgamate with the Secondary Modern School at Over-Ross, and was re-named the John Kyrle High School in 1979. Private hire was also part of the business that I understand ceased to exist somewhere around 1989. His last bus, a 29-seater Bedford OB registration MEM38 is now safely preserved in the Martin Perry collection at Shobdon, north Herefordshire.

Another almost forgotten venture was the Broad Oak coach company jointly owned by Alfie Benjamin, a Garway farmer, and Mr Arthur

FAW 620 is the 1949 Bedford OB which Percy Tummey purchased from Evason Coaches in June 1951. It was sold to Broad Oak Coach Company in March 1961 and then to Don Nicholls in April 1967. (Joan Tummey)

Illingworth who owned the small garage and petrol station at Broad Oak from about 1958 until 1978. In 1967 their bus was sold to Don Nicholls together with the school contract. This bus was a Bedford OB coach, registration number FAW 620 that was purchased from Percy Tummey of Llangarron in March 1961.

Graham Nicholls, a grandson of Ellen Nicholls, who bought the garage from Arthur Illingworth in 1978, was another bus operator between the years 1969 to 1995. His father, who started with Hereford Transport Company became a bus conductor, then a driver as a long serving employee of the Red and White Bus Company. Graham is well known for his Saturday morning shopping trips to Ross-on-Wye. Driving through Garway and over the Hill, he collected the shoppers, delivered them to Ross and at the end of the morning brought them all back with their heavy bags and dropped them off as near their houses as possible. A much-appreciated service! In 1995, H&H coaches took over this route for a short time. Although no longer a coach operator, Graham and his family still run the substantial garage, filling station and shop business at Broad Oak.

In 1956 Kingstone School with its newly acquired prefab classrooms became a secondary modern. Consequently the children from Garway who had not passed their 11 plus exam were transferred to there and thus Garway became just a primary school. Transport to the school was provided by a Wye Valley Motors bus garaged at Pontrilas. The route ran through St Weonards, Wormelow, Tram Inn and on to Kingstone. Due to overcrowding on the bus, this was discontinued and a separate route was devised with the Garway children being taken through Kentchurch, Pontrilas, Wormbridge and then to Kingstone.

In the '60s a bus owned by Mr Eric Smith of the Red Lion, Kilpeck, took children from Orcop to Kingstone School. It was driven by Mr Bill Watkins of Wormbridge who also worked in the timber trade. Tragedy struck on 8 September 1971 when a rope snapped whilst he was loading a timber carriage resulting in him, at 40 years of age, being crushed by a tree trunk. Gethin Nicholls of Wormelow then drove his bus on the Kilpeck to Garway School run from 1972 until the early 1990s. He started up with a 41-seater SB Bedford coach purchased from Charlie Bounds' Golden Wings Coaches of Maylord Street, Hereford. His brother, Graham Nicholls, conveyed the Orcop children through Bagwyllydiart to St Weonards Primary School from 1970 to 1995.

Another of the Nicholls family is Don who started out in business as a young man in April 1967 with a 29-seater Bedford OB coach, registration number FAW 620 previously mentioned in this chapter. The bus was available for private hire but the mainstay of his business was carrying children from the Garway area to Ross Grammar School, picking up along the way while Les Gardiner was covering the Garway Hill route. Don's journey was timed to meet with the Wye Valley Motors by Miss Lawrence's post office in Garway to cater for the Kentchurch children. In addition he would take the Garway School children to their weekly swimming lessons in Ross-on-Wye. At one stage Don had three buses on the road and was the favourite choice of Garway Womens Institute for their social outings. He was invariably told that the trip started half an hour before it really did just to make sure that he was on time. Don's timekeeping was legendary!

In 2004 his remaining coach and contract was sold to H&H coaches. Now, some 40 years on from when he started, Don is driving for Phil Jones Coaches of Burley Gate mainly on PGL transport, and on Sundays for Martin Perry of Bromyard.

At the present time H&H Coaches of Ross-on-Wye have the Garway to Kingstone contract. They also serve the Garway to Monmouth schools using a Hopper. Occasionally a Hopper bus belonging to 'David Field coaches' of Newent performs this duty. Incidentally, the rather enigmatic H&H stands for Mike Horlick and Malcolm Harris. For the children the route to school was not always straightforward. Up until 1974, when Wye Valley Motors sold out to Yeomans of Canon Pyon, there were children from the Kentchurch area travelling as far as Garway before transferring to the 'Red & White' Abergavenny to Ross bus for the completion of their lengthy journey to Ross Grammar School. The transport needs of Garway School are now met by Phil Jones Coaches which take pupils to their swimming classes at Ross-on-Wye.

In these days of low profit margins and short-term public service contracts of just three years, operating a bus service has become a very challenging and competitive business.

Extracts from Kellys' *Directories* of Herefordshire

Garway

1922   The Hereford Transport Co. Ltd. run omnibuses to Abergavenny, tues; to Hereford wed. & sat.; to Ross thurs. & to Monmouth, fri. & alternate mon.

1926   The Hereford Transport Co. Ltd. run omnibuses to Abergavenny, tues; to Hereford, wed. & sat; to Ross, thurs. & to Monmouth, fri. & alternate mon. The Midland Omnibus Co. run omnibuses to Monmouth, alternate mon. (market days); to Hereford, wed. & sat; to Ross-on-Wye, thur. & to Abergavenny, tues. & fri. The ' Northgate' omnibus runs to Monmouth alternate mon.; to Abergavenny, tues. & sat.; to Hereford, wed. & to Ross-on-Wye thurs. & sat.

1929   The 'Red and White' omnibus service between Ross & Abergavenny passes through Broad Oak daily. The 'Northgate' omnibus runs to Monmouth alternate mon.; to Abergavenny, tues. & sat.; to Hereford wed. & Ross-on-Wye, thurs. & sat.

1934   The 'Jardins Motor' services between Ross & Abergavenny passes through Broad Oak daily & to Hereford, wed.

1941   The 'Jardins Motors' service between Ross & Abergavenny passes through Broad Oak daily & to Hereford on wed

   (The entries for 1934 and 1941 are puzzling. I could find no record of a bus operator by the name of Jardin so presumably it should have been Jorden. However, this leads to another puzzle as by 1937 Jordens had been taken over by Red and White Services.)

11   White Rocks

'We've come to see the White Rocks'. A couple of tourists had pulled up in their car outside White Rocks House and were frantically consulting their O.S. map. Almost apologetically, I directed them back up the road to the turning that would take them up to Rock Mount, the house near to where the boulders lie. They aren't that enormous and they aren't at all white, but there is an impressive spill of rocks which form a damp and mossy grotto that has something of the Victorian Gothic about it. Legend has it that the rocks were left here by Jack O'Kent and the Devil when, for some undoubtedly nefarious reason, they were using the boulders to build a dam at nearby Orcop, but dropped them on the eastern slopes of Garway Hill, creating the White Rocks from which the hamlet takes its name.

Mr and Mrs Elmsley, friends of Miss Waters of White Rocks House, investigating the actual White Rocks boulders during the early 1900s

The small hamlet of White Rocks comprises about a dozen scattered houses of varying size and age. Such is the gradient of the slope and the contour of the land that one can have a near neighbour and yet not be visually aware of their presence. Being private and communal at the same time, it attracts people who love its seclusion and beauty; people who love having the glorious Garway Hill in their backyard. The first people to enjoy White Rocks were probably an Iron Age family. Archaeologists have long known of a site, dating from that era, beside the track that leads from the top end of Sun Lane to the summit of Garway Hill. This site has subsequently been subjected to exploratory excavation in June 2006 (see Chapter 4). In addition to this another smaller site clearly showed up in recent aerial photography, but was not included in the planned excavation. The Romans knew the place too, having constructed an auxiliary fort below White Rocks in a field between the Garway to Pontrilas Road and the river Monnow which was excavated in 1986 by the Monmouthshire Archaeological Society. There may have been a settlement at White Rocks itself as early as the 11th century. There are records of a 'salt ley', that is a route along which salt traders travelled, passing through White Rocks en route from Worcester to the White Castle in Monmouthshire. These were the 'white men' and their routes are littered with etymological reminders of their transit: White House, Whitwick Manor, Whitestone, Whitcliffe, Whitney and so on. The name could also refer to the quarrying that went on here in the post-medieval period. There is limestone on the hill as well as the underlying red sandstone, and limestone is often called 'white rock' as in the famous White Rocks cliffs of County Antrim in Northern Ireland, White Rocks Quarries in Florida or the White Rock near Martinborough on the North Island of New Zealand. Some authorities believe that, in medieval times, the community at White Rocks was larger than that of nearby Garway village. If true, this may well have been because of its situation on a trading route. Nowadays, there is not much passing traffic but White Rocks is on the Herefordshire Trail, the 154-mile walking trail that begins and ends at the Market House in Ledbury, circumnavigating the county along its borders.

Geographically, White Rocks is situated in a comfortable fold of Garway Hill, facing east and south. Only the inhabitants of Little Adawent and Little Castlefield can watch the sun as it sinks in the west. It is sheltered from the prevailing winds which whistle overhead. The soil is acid and fertile. Gardening here is a struggle to stop things growing; saplings of ash and hazel take root at the drop of a hat. The pervasive bracken of Garway Hill encroaches right up to the garden walls. Ferns, mosses and lichens are abundant. Lawns stay green in the hottest summer even when the land round about has turned a yellow-ochre reminiscent of Tuscany. On clear nights the sky is sprinkled with stars and dusted by the Milky Way. In the lanes the tiny luminescent green lights of glow-worms can be seen — vivid in June, dim by August when most of the mating has taken place and the larval ardour diminished. There are many species of butterfly — including the now rare Green Fritillary. The white horses of Garway Hill descend from the higher pastures at night to drink from its springs. Just outside White Rocks House is a massive Sweet Chestnut tree, strangely elevated on a stony tump. Now several hundred years old, it was probably a boundary tree, marking the limits of an estate. It stands in the old Victorian orchard of White Rocks House affording shelter to the wandering sheep.

White Rocks House in the early 1900s. Garway Hill appears in the background much less shrouded in trees than it does now

Most of the houses at White Rocks date from around 1820 or just before. Certainly, most of the existing cottages are in evidence on the 1840 tithe map of the area. There are many stories about past inhabitants of White Rocks, some true, others based on a glimmer of truth but embellished by decades of Chinese Whispers. White Rocks House, which is architecturally a 'Streatham Villa' — a design of house which was popular in the London suburbs in the late 19th century — was built in the 1880s on the site of an earlier and more modest abode. In its Victorian form, it was first inhabited by Eleanor Waters and Mary Warburton Waters, mother and daughter, who moved here from a salubrious villa in Hampstead, London. Eleanor's roots were in Kilpeck. She had moved to London, married an art dealer and had enjoyed a very comfortable social existence of tea and concert parties. Widowed and in her late 60s she moved back to Herefordshire with her spinster daughter, Mary. They must have been the first of the many 'in-comers' who have since moved into the predominately farming community. Even now White Rocks can feel quite remote, but in Victorian times it must have seemed at the end of the earth. The Waters ladies lived at White Rocks House with a local servant girl, Mary Holly, otherwise known as Polly Molly Holly. Jesse, Polly's sister, helped too and a male gardener tended the garden and looked after the pony. Popular legend has it that Mary was a strident Suffragette who was banished to this area by her brothers who wanted rid of her. Another story suggests she was a bit of a drinker. Originally, there was a large bell on the roof of White Rocks House which was linked to chained bell-pulls in each room. Supposedly, the bell could be rung if the lady of the house needed assistance after a tipple too many.

The servants of White Rocks House probably snapped by amateur photographer Miss Waters. The servant in the foreground is probably Mary Holly (Polly Molly) who later inherited the house from her mistress

The Suffragette story is certainly not true. That rumour probably arose because Mary's sister was a Mrs Pankhurst. However, she was not the Emmeline Pankhurst of 'Votes for Women' fame, but Ada, who had married a Covent Garden fruit merchant called Dilnot Dibley Pankhurst. The surname was probably enough to stimulate local imaginations and wagging tongues; in such a way local myths are born and passed on. No-one can know if the rumours of alcoholism were true. The presence of a large bell on a remote country house was actually also fairly common. What better way in pre-telephone days of summoning help, especially when the household was largely female? We can get a flavour of what life was like at White Rocks in the late Victorian period from the many photographs which survive — thanks, probably, to Mary Waters' pioneering interest in amateur photography. It was a genteel era of tea in the garden, servants struggling with the laundry, friends arriving by horse and trap, sailor-suited boys in the orchard, lives shared with much-loved dogs, ponies and dairy cows. White Rocks has never been a place to attract those who follow convention. Mary Waters certainly did not follow the social etiquettes of the day when she took up her Kodak box camera or when, on her death, she bequeathed White Rocks House, Rocks Bottom and Little Adawent cottages (all of which by then she owned), to her faithful servant, Mary Holly. It's a rags to riches story worthy

Miss Waters and Polly Molly going off on a jaunt in pony and trap attended by the gentleman who probably looked after the garden and the horse and who would have lived in the tiny cottage adjacent to the main house

of a Catherine Cookson novel. Mary was from a poor family and had been one of 12 children. Some of her family had left the area to find a better life and religious fulfilment as pioneer Mormons in Salt Lake City, Utah. Mary Holly lived at White Rocks House until 1943 where she died, apparently having spent her latter years berating imaginary passers-by in the lane.

To the west and east of White Rocks House respectively are Little Adawent and Rocks Bottom. Little Adawent had at one time a neighbour in a larger house called Hadwent. This house has now disappeared apart from some stones still lying in the adjacent field. Little Adawent first belonged to a family by the name of Maddox. In his will of 1820, Thomas Maddox bequeathed the cottage to his wife, Mary, for the duration of her life and then to his son, James, with a bequest of 'six live sheep and one new bed' to be given to his daughter, Sarah. The giving of beds in wills was obviously still as important and as common as it had been two hundred years earlier when Shakespeare left his wife, Anne Hathaway, his 'second best bed'. James Maddox, when he inherited, struggled to keep up his mortgage payments, ran up a lot of debt, and eventually sold in 1859 for the princely sum of £150. It is interesting to note that property investment was not in those days a way to make a fortune, as is often the case now. When Little Adawent was sold in 1931,

113

72 years later, its selling price had gone down to £145! The lack of a hike in the purchase price for many years is partly due to the house sale happening during the Depression, as well as the fact that it had, probably, during all those years remained a simple unmodernised cottage. Indeed, when the present occupants bought Little Adawent in 1994 the then owner still fetched her water daily from a nearby spring which she filtered through sand. Her shower was a magnificent Heath-Robinson affair comprising a small tank (kept on the windowsill in an upstairs room), attached to a tube which channelled water downstairs into a watering can rose. To shower, one (simply) heated some water on the gas cooker, poured it into the upstairs tank, opened a tap on the tank and then ran downstairs to the lean-to and stood in a tin bath underneath the shower rose. Prior to that, the cottage had been occupied since 1931 by one of the many Mrs Powells of White Rocks. 'Fat Mrs Powell' of Little Adawent was well-known for keeping ferrets down her front. In contrast, 'Thin Mrs Powell' lived in Rocks Bottom.. The third Mrs Powell was Emily who lived at Little Castlefield and was an antecedent of the family who currently live on the farm.

North of White Rocks House on the opposite side of the lane is a ruin which was still inhabited until the 1950s and was the home of the Williams family. Its name was originally White Rocks Cottage and was a separate dwelling that had been occupied by Alfred Williams, his wife and two daughters since 1930. (This cottage is not to be confused with the White Rocks Cottage which now exists on White Rocks Road closer to Little Garway Farm. This was a later construction.) Mr Williams must have cut an alarming figure to the young children of White Rocks wearing, as he did, a black patch over the ear he had lost during the First World War. Just before the Second World War there had been plans to renovate the cottage with a grant from the local council, but the materials had been withdrawn on the outbreak of hostilities. This withdrawal of potential investment before the war also affected Little Adawent. As a result White Rocks Cottage was in a very poor state of repair in the post-war period. Mr Williams had been promised alternative accommodation by Herefordshire Council, but unfortunately he went into hospital in 1950 and died before it could be granted. His two daughters, who had lived at White Rocks with him, applied to the council for the promised house but were refused on the grounds that the promise had been made to their father, not to them. Several resignations from the council followed in protest at the injustice of this decision, but the girls did not get their house. One week after the girls moved out, the side wall of White Rocks Cottage collapsed. It has been a ruin ever since and its land was incorporated with White Rocks House.

The Grange may have the oldest origins of any of the buildings at White Rocks. It is thought that it had commenced life in the 16th century as a cider mill. Certainly, within living memory, the area was a mass of cider apple orchards and it was not unusual for a small community to have its own centre for the crushing and pressing of cider apples. The original cider mill of the Grange has been added to over the years, making it a large imposing building. It enjoyed an alternative existence for a while in the 1970s when it was a centre for meditation and retreats.

The Chantry, in its present form, was built in 1911 by a retired vicar. It seems that this cottage was built on the site of an earlier religious building called St Gabriel's Chantry that was listed as uninhabited in the 1891 census and is thought to date from the medieval period. This would add weight to the idea that there was indeed a medieval settlement at White Rocks. Chantries were an important part of English Catholicism and were usually endowed by rich people or even members of craftsman guilds who would employ a priest to pray for their souls after death. This may suggest that a person (or persons) of some substance lived in or near White Rocks during medieval times. It is also interesting that the Chantry was dedicated to the Archangel Gabriel who is associated with power and might. Gabriel is also the messenger, the angel who brought the news of Christ's birth to the shepherds. The idea of a messenger angel presiding over the chapel would also fit in with White Rocks being on an old trade route. The Chantry may well have been neglected or even damaged in the mid-16th century when Anglican reformers tried to eradicate all signs of Catholicism. Remembering its past history, the 20th-century vicar incorporated the Gothic style chapel windows into the house and used one room as a small private chapel. If the Chantry was once used as a place to pray for the eternal well-being of guildsmen it is probably well suited to its present owner who is a renowned silversmith. In the 1950s it was inhabited by the sister of the local Member of Parliament for South Herefordshire, James Purdon Lewes Thomas, who was later to achieve ministerial status and became First Lord of the Admiralty. He obviously carried some influence at the seat of power because, not only did he advise Anthony Eden during the Suez crisis but he also brought about a significant development at White Rocks. The said Honourable Member took it upon himself to raise a question in Parliament regarding the lack of milk at White Rocks and the effect it was having on the several infants and children who then lived in the hamlet. Cadburys factory in Bournville near Birmingham bought up all the milk produced on the farms in the area and none was left for the locals. The political intervention was discussed in the House and brought results as a milk delivery was very soon arranged. Much to the inhabitants' dismay, the milk came from a farm near Orcop which, it was said, was not known for its cleanliness. The local children always referred to it as 'dirty milk'.

The Chantry, Chantry Cottage and the group of houses at Hillside are the only houses at White Rocks which have mains water. This was achieved in the early 1980s when the inhabitants of the cottages decided that they would dig their own trench across Garway Hill Common so that the Water Board could connect them to the mains supply that ran along the Garway to Bagwyllyddiart Road. It was a major undertaking involving many hours of blood, sweat and tears. Luckily, despite the geological nature of the hill, the trench was accomplished without hitting rocky outcrops that would have probably put paid to the enterprise.

A past inhabitant who lived in White Rocks House as a young child just after the Second World War, remembers White Rocks as being less gentrified than it is now. She recalls very run-down houses and rutted tracks. She says that, just beyond White Rocks House, was a rubbish tip where locals would dump unwanted items. The protection of places of natural beauty was not then high on the political agenda. She also remembers the fields beyond the second cattle grid being a mass of white rabbits' tails of an evening, which, if you clapped your hands would scatter in all directions; such was the size of the rabbit population before myxomatosis. Red squirrels were also then in evidence. White

Rocks Farm, now a smart holiday home, was just a run down barn. Many of the other cottages would, in modern terms, have been described as ripe for improvement. Even so, she remembers it as the perfect place to spend a childhood although her teenage sisters were less enamoured. It remains an idyllic spot that can bewitch its inhabitants. It's a hard-to-leave place. The lady mentioned above showed us her mother's diary entry for the day her family left their house in 1955 which reads: 'Farewell to darling White Rocks House'. At the time of writing we have only lived in White Rocks House for a year and, in that time, no less than three past inhabitants have made a pilgrimage back to our idiosyncratic front door. There is certainly something magical about the place. There is a timelessness about White Rocks which probably has much to do with the continuity provided by the farming families, most of whom have lived on the hill for generations be it at Old Garden Farm, Little Castlefield or Little Garway. Those who have lived at White Rocks have always lived alongside sheep and have enjoyed the annual rite of lambing every spring and the bleating of ewes and their young throughout the early summer. No matter how many new faces come and go, the place will always belong to them.

12　The Methodists and the Mormons

The Methodists

The Primitive Methodist Chapel on Garway Hill was built in 1860 on a small triangular plot of land which had been allotted to Abraham Baker under the Enclosure Act. The Bakers were an old Orcop family and Abraham had managed to acquire a substantial amount of land under the Act. A lane, which connects the roads that run either side of the chapel, is still known locally as Baker's Lane. His granddaughter married William Rowlands and it was he who conveyed the land and for which '£5 was paid for consideration money.' The building was made of local stone with a slate roof and false chimney and could hold a congregation of 130 people. It was officially opened for worship on Sunday, 30 September 1860, and was full to capacity inside with many more standing outside in the Chapel yard. The following day a tea-meeting was held with around 300 people in attendance. Previous to this the Primitive Methodists had held their services at Pennywink, Bagwyllydiart and for many years there had also been regular meetings for worship, on a Sunday evening, in a house at Orcop Hill, on the other side of the parish. They also met at each other's homes and had open-air meetings for want of somewhere more suitable, but with swelling membership the need for their own premises had become a necessity. There had been much religious fervour in the area when the Mormon missionary work was at its peak in the 1840s but by the late 1850s most of the converts to the new faith had already emigrated. Those who chose to remain now had no real sense of belonging and many probably joined the increasingly popular Methodists.

In those early years they were preached to by one of many travelling preachers who belonged to what was known as the Hereford Circuit. A preacher's plan for the circuit was published showing locations and times of services and the name of the preacher in attendance. There were also certain regulations to be adhered to:

> **First** No Person is allowed to preach among us unless authorized by, and subject to the Circuit Authorities.
> **Second** Any Preacher who neglects an appointment, or to publish, or to make Collections, or lead Class, where planned to do so shall, for the First and Second neglects be admonished, and for the Third be removed from the Plan.
> **Third** No Tea Meeting must be held without the sanction of the quarterly meeting.
> **Fourth** All our members are respectfully requested to subscribe their Class-pence Weekly, according to rule.

In those earlier times there were three services on a Sunday — morning, afternoon and evening — with the most staunch of followers attending all three. Youngsters were also encouraged to attend these.

Despite a fall in numbers over the years, regular services continued to be held on a Sunday afternoon as well as the occasional christening, wedding or funeral. With such a close knit community the latter often drawing a large attendance, with people standing in the yard and at the roadside, bringing a temporary halt to traffic whilst the service took place. As congregations began to dwindle further there were fewer children and the last Sunday School was held in the 1960s. This had been run for many years by Agnes Davies and Mrs Smith. In the mid-1900s there were Sunday School picnics held up on the hill close to the home of Mrs Eva Smith at Belle Vue Farm. One of the memorable things from Sunday School were the cards which were given out each week that you attended. These attendance cards were saved up to be exchanged for either a prize or a book.

Each year there would be an eagerly looked forward to 'Sunday School outing' with trips to places like Porthcawl and Aberystwyth — Did it always rain in Aberystwyth? But the favourite destination and the one most frequented, was Barry Island. It had it all — community singing on the beach with the Salvation Army, donkey rides, crazy golf, the funfair and Fortes ice cream. A few heady rides at the fair always finished off the day before heading back to the bus. This may have been the only trip to the seaside that some had during the year and there was always some tale to tell: getting lost on the overcrowded beach, surprise at how they had caught the sun, or the embarrassment of having to ask the driver to stop on the long journey home so they could nip behind the hedge. It was all part of the fun and made for a good day out.

A chapel anniversary sometime in the early 1900s

Another big event on the Chapel calendar was the annual Anniversary in which members of the Sunday School would recite or sing. It was an occasion for dressing in the Sunday best clothes as this would be a performance in front of a packed audience of parents, grandparents, aunts and uncles — an evening of high tension for both participants and audience alike. The closing of the Sunday School brought an end to events like this. The following celebration from years gone by was recorded in an article, possibly from a *Hereford Times* or *Journal*, of the day.

PRIMITIVE METHODIST CHAPEL ANNIVERSARY

Situate on the brow of the northern slope of Garway Hill – or, geographically, mountain, and overlooking a beautiful landscape of South Herefordshire scenery, is the quiet little Zion of the Primitive Methodists of that district. From this spot, which is hundreds of feet above the sea level, glimpses of the 'lovely Malvern hills' and many other interesting heights are caught; and it seems gratifying to the members to think that their predecessors should have built their chapel in such a lofty and commanding position, insomuch that its elevation evokes a feeling of reverential awe in the passer-by. However, Sunday week was the appointed day to celebrate the opening of this much needed and only chapel, which from 1860, the year of its erection, has been the means of bettering both the moral and social condition of the people of that scattered neighbourhood. Two good evangelical sermons were preached by Mr William Powell (Llanrosser, Hay) in the afternoon and evening respectively. On Monday the usual tea-meeting was held, and the weather being so favourable for the in-gathering of the grain, the number scarcely reached the average attendance of previous years. Notwithstanding this unavoidable drawback, the evening's proceedings were not less enjoyable; and a comfortable company sat down to the tables, and received much kindness and attention from those who busily engaged in the preparation of a well provided tea. Mrs Manning, Ridway Farm; Mrs Bevan, Old Orchards; Mrs Badham, Hawthorn Wells; and Miss Nellie Morgan, Garway Hill, presided at the tables, and were greatly assisted by Mrs Sayce, Old House Farm; Miss Rowlands and Mr Beavan. Gifts of milk and butter were gratefully received from Mrs Lewis, High Gardens, and Mrs Johnson, Brooks Farm. The chapel was tastefully and prettily adorned with a few of the last flowers of summer, which added considerably to the pleasure of the visitors. The decorations were carried out by Mrs Badham and Miss Nellie Morgan. The interval following tea offered an excellent opportunity for a ramble on the summit, which is only a few hundred yards distant; and a few availed themselves of the gratification attending the view of rural scenery, particularly such as greets the eye from Garway Mountain.

In the evening following this there was a public meeting where various issues were discussed relating to Methodism in general.

Harvest Festival Sunday saw the chapel decorated with flowers, fruit and vegetables, which were auctioned for charity after a second service on the following evening. Owing to a fall in congregation numbers there is no longer a Monday service and in the last few years the chapel is just decorated with flowers for the Harvest Sunday.

On the evening prior to the harvest service, all generations took part in the polishing and trimming and tying up of the produce. Even the coat pegs on the wall, either side of the chapel, were adorned with offerings tied on with string or raffia. On one occasion Mr Eynon was the cause of a fit of giggling when, for want of somewhere to lay his hat, placed it atop a large cabbage on the windowcill! (On a wet Sunday afternoon, those who were unfortunate enough to find themselves sitting at the wall end of the pew, below a pile of dripping coats and hats hung on the pegs, may have wished they had chosen somewhere a little drier. Nowadays, with the advantage of just stepping out of a motor vehicle and a quick dash inside with the aid of an umbrella, the pegs are seldom used. Long gone are the days of wrapping up and braving the elements to walk a couple of miles to chapel.)

To bring a more youthful note to services, occasionally, when it became Mr Les Rowlands' turn to preach, members of the Garway Youth group would come along and perform, singing and playing instruments. Les (a descendant of William Rowlands who had conveyed the land for the chapel) and his wife, Fay, have run the youth group from their home in Garway for over 30 years.

It was during the 1960s that electricity was laid on for lighting and heating and later when funds allowed, concrete paths were laid in the chapel yard. In more recent years steps were provided to reach the lower road and an additional path was laid along to the 'top' and 'bottom' road intersection. There are many who have fond memories of swinging on the railings which run along the roadside, and returning home with grazed knees and grass stained skirts and trousers.

Nowadays the chapel falls within the Cwm and District Methodist Circuit. Life-long member Meg Brown has been a regular organist and kept the chapel accounts. A service is held on a fortnightly basis with a small but regular attendance, and are taken either by the Minister, Rev Gordon Tonge, or by lay preachers from around the district. Money is raised for the upkeep of the chapel by holding various events during the year. A Christmas Bazaar held at Ewyas Harold, usually in November, sees the various chapels within the circuit coming together for a joint event. This is where the Christmas mistletoe is bought and those many bargains for presents and stocking fillers.

With so many small chapels around the country, from all denominations, now falling into disuse, it is good to see that Garway Hill Primitive Methodist Chapel is still being supported.

The Church of Jesus Christ of Latter-day Saints

In 1823, a young man, Joseph Smith, had a vision. In it he was visited by an angel named Moroni, telling him of an ancient record containing God's dealings with the former inhabitants of the American continent. In 1827, Joseph retrieved this record, which was inscribed on thin golden plates, and began translating its words by the 'gift of God.' The resulting manuscript, the *Book of Mormon*, was published in March 1830. On 6 April 1830 in Fayette, New York, Joseph Smith organized The Church of Jesus Christ of Latter-day Saints with just six members and became its first president.

It is hard to imagine that an emerging religion in America could within a little over a decade have reached a small community in a remote corner of Herefordshire, but that

James Bevan, the first convert to leave Garway Hill. (Courtesy Daughters of Utah Pioneer)

is exactly what happened when Joseph Smith sent out his Apostles to recruit. Much has been written about events that took place in the north of our county but in the last few years research has shown that Garway Hill also had an important role in the history of the Mormon Church in this country.

On 24 July 1847, Brigham Young reached the Salt Lake Valley and uttered those now famous words: 'This is the place'. By 28 July, just four days later, a small group from the sick detachment of the Mormon Battalion entered the valley, amongst them 26-year-old James Bevan whose family home was Middle Moors Farm, Garway Hill. Amongst a group of less than 500 men women and children he became one of the first settlers of what was later to become Salt Lake City. This first community lived in self-imposed isolation; the territory they inhabited was still part of Mexico. The Mormon state was firstly called 'Deseret' but a few years later in 1850, after the Mexican–American War, the 'State of Deseret' was absorbed by the rapidly growing United States of America and it became the Territory of Utah. It was not, however, until 1890 when Church President, Wilford Woodruff, ended polygamy that Utah was finally admitted to the Union and in 1896 it became the 45th State. Families and single men and women from Herefordshire were amongst some of the very first pioneers to settle this land and William Carter from Ledbury 'broke the first ground and laid the first furrow' in the valley. It is extraordinary that such an event has remained as an untold history until recent years, but with the current interest in family history and the advantages of internet access the stories of these adventurers are now beginning to be heard.

It was at a time when life was exceedingly hard, after the change and upheaval of the Enclosure Act, that the voice of hope was spoken to the receptive ears of those struggling to make an existence in a harsh landscape. Although the new religion had first been brought to these shores in 1837, the first Apostles remained almost exclusively in the Lancashire area. It was only when charismatic church leader Wilford Woodruff, on a visit from America,

Wilford Woodruff who brought the Mormon faith to Herefordshire. (LDS Church History Library and Archives)

heard of a family named Benbow in Herefordshire who might listen sympathetically to his preachings that they ventured this far south. He arrived at the Benbow farm at Castle Frome in March 1840 and within days had begun to convert both family and friends, one being Thomas Kington, the local superintendent of the United Brethren, a religious group to which John Benbow belonged. They had broken away from the Methodists and in 1836 had built themselves a chapel at Gadfield Elm on the Herefordshire / Gloucestershire border. (Almost the entire congregation of the United Brethren were converted and the chapel was deeded to the Mormon Church. When the time came to emigrate the chapel was sold to assist with funds and it later fell into disrepair. In recent years it has been restored and is the oldest surviving Mormon chapel in the world. It houses a museum where some of the Garway Mormon history is on display.)

During the hot, dry spring of 1840, James Morgan, whilst working in that area, heard these new teachings and was converted and ordained a priest of The Church of Jesus Christ of The Latter-day Saints. He was already a senior member of the United Brethren church but had become much disillusioned. By May of that year, both he and Margaret Morgan, who was working as a governess for the Hill family at Pitthouse Farm, Dymock, had embraced the new faith and brought it to the Morgan home at Little Garway Farm, White Rocks. In June, James himself baptised 11 people at Little Garway and the home was made open to visiting missionaries. Noted in the minutes of a conference held at Stanley Hall, Castle Frome on 21 June 1840, is the first record we have of the Garway branch, just three months after the arrival of Woodruff in Herefordshire: '... together with a small branch of Little Garway of Twelve Members, One Priest, and One Teacher.'

The month of June also saw the arrival of James Palmer, a recent convert from The United Brethren Church, to Garway Hill and Orcop, where he had been sent to carry on the good works. It is because of the detailed diaries that Palmer and others kept that we have a clear picture of their missionary work in this area, and also an insight into what living and working conditions were like at that time. Most of the people were just cottagers living in small 'two up, two down' houses, with a few hens, a pig to fatten for the bacon and perhaps a cow for milking. In addition there would be a small vegetable garden to tend and maybe a few fruit trees. Life was a constant struggle and the winter of 1840 was particularly hard. It had been a poor harvest and many crops had failed, there was only just enough food to share around and morale was at an all time low. It was at this most desperate time in their lives that they began to hear of a new life with a chance to succeed, not just to exist but to have a future to look forward too. When faced with the everyday poverty and hardship they were enduring, the promise of this new life in a far away land must have felt like an answer to their prayers.

Palmer worked tirelessly, walking long distances, preaching morning, afternoon and evening sometimes alone, often with visiting missionaries from America. Services were held in various homes on the hill and baptisms took place in local springs, ponds and the river Monnow. At the peak of this religious activity, during one week, there had been a total of 12 teachers and preachers working in this district. Using Garway Hill as a base they travelled to places as far afield as Longtown, Crickhowell, Monmouth and Abergavenny, very often to a relative of someone from the hill where they might be assured of a warm welcome. Often they were provided with a much welcomed meal and perhaps a bed for the night. The importance of the missionary work in this area can be seen in the following extract from *Times and Seasons*, November 1840. This was a newspaper published fortnightly, in Nauvoo, Illinois, to chronicle the efforts and spread the message of the works of the Church:

> Elder William Donaldson, member of the army bound for East Indies, writes from Chatham 24th July – 'We go on board tomorrow. I have had a glorious vision about going into the land of Egypt.'
> Elders Woodruff and Smith write from Herefordshire, August 3rd – 'Things are more favourable in Garway. New doors are opening in that country, and they want a labourer there. We wish Elder Wilding would go into that region soon, if he is going.

On Wilford Woodruff's visit to Garway Hill in 1841 he was made most welcome at the Little Garway household and stayed on the farm between the 5 and 9 March. In his diary he wrote:

> March 5, 1841 ... took Breakfast with Mr Maston and walked 10 miles through mud and water in the midst of a driving March rain storm to Sister Morgan at little Garway, where I found a plesent [*sic*] family of the Saints. We were drenched with rain, but we found a good fire and spent the day comfortable. In the evening I had an interview with Elder Littlewood.
> March 6, 1841 ... I spent the Day at Sister Morgans reading the history of Rome which was truly interesting ...
> March 7, 1841 ... Sunday, I preached in the morning at the home of Br.Thomas Root and in the evening at the Kitchen, upon the Book of Mormon had a full house.
> March 8, 1841 ... I met in the Garway Conference at the Kitchen. Elder Levi Richards was chosen president and Elder James Morgan clerk.

It is said that Woodruff was so impressed with the fireplaces he saw over here that he had one installed in every room at his Nauvoo house, Illinois! In the spring of 2007, Richard Woodruff Lambert and Wilford Woodruff from Salt Lake, both direct descendants, visited Herefordshire as part of a trip following in the footsteps of their ancestor. They were thrilled to have the opportunity to be photographed alongside the newly restored fireplace at Little Garway where Wilford senior had warmed himself all those years ago.

The Kitchen, Garway Hill, or Old Kitchen as it is now known, the home of

Richard Woodruff Lambert and Wilford Woodruff beside the fireplace at Little Garway Farm

123

Thomas Arthur, was where the Conference meetings were now being held. It was officially formed on 6 April 1841, with Elder Levi Richards as its President. When Woodruff himself preached here in 1841, there were present: a High Priest, a High Counsel travelling, seven Elders, eleven Priests, two Teachers, a Deacon and a gathering of 134 members. Writing in that same year he states:

> The excitement upon the subject in the city of Hereford has been so great, that it has assembled together in the Market place 3,000 persons at a time to hear something upon the cause of the Latter Day Saints.

By 1842 the Garway Conference, as it was called, was an important part of the Mormon movement in Britain. (Liverpool had 570 members, London 400, Birmingham 309, and Garway 197).

Over the next 30 years many of the hill community packed their belongings, as much as they needed and could afford to take, then set off from either Liverpool or Bristol for the east coast of America. After facing much unrest and turmoil the Church headquarters moved from New York to Ohio, then to Missouri and later to Illinois where in 1839 they established the community of Nauvoo. This site was carved out of a tract of swampland bordering the Mississippi River. Under Joseph Smith's leadership the swamps were drained and building work began, creating houses, farms and businesses. This is where the first early Garway Hill converts began to set up home and were able to use their skills as stonemasons, carpenters and builders to begin to create a new life for themselves. Some of them worked on the building of the Temple which they later had to abandon. But by 1844 the population had swelled enough to rival Chicago. Its political power began to cause fear and distrust in the neighbouring communities. Mobs began to attack settlements, burned the crops and homes and threatened the people. Church leader, Joseph Smith, after incarceration in Nauvoo Jail was murdered and Brigham Young became the second President of the Saints. He knew they would yet again have to move and began to plan a mass migration to the west.

Nauvoo Temple, Illinois, c.1846. The first converts from Garway Hill would have contributed financially and helped with the construction. (LDS Church History Library and Archives)

Thousands sold their land and homes and made arrangements to leave. The exodus was run like a military operation, one hundred pioneer families in a group, each with a covered wagon, commanded by a leader. Milking cows, beef cattle and sheep were taken, in order that they could start farming when they reached their destination. The Mississippi River was crossed on rafts or small flat boats, but later on when it froze the wagons crossed on the ice. Brigham Young's group left in February 1846 and their journey was to take more than a year. They travelled through deep snow and the wagons offered little protection against the freezing cold winds. By spring they had deep mud to contend with and exhausted travellers had to make roads and fall timber to make bridges to enable them to cross rivers. By the following winter, the groups had gathered at a place by the Missouri River, which they called Winter Quarters. Here they built a thousand log cabins, but food was in such short supply that many fell ill and died. In the spring of 1847, Young's group of 143 men, 3 women and 2 children set off alone, mapping out the trail as they went for those who were to follow later; not until July did they reach what would become their permanent home. Amongst them were some of those early pioneers from Herefordshire.

Every pioneer had a different story to tell but the trials and tribulations and tales of hardships that they suffered were universal. The journey undertaken by those who left Garway Hill was an experience way beyond any other they had endured and far more than the imagination could allow for. The long sea journey, the bitterly cold weather, disease and the threat of attack from both wild animals and Native Indians became a part of daily life. It was the strength of character of these people who had lived and worked the common land that enabled them to survive these ordeals where others fell by the wayside. Unlike their city counter-

BILL OF PARTICULARS

FOR THE EMIGRANTS LEAVING THIS GOVERN-
MENT NEXT SPRING.

Each family consisting of five persons, to be provided with

1 good strong wagon, well covered with a light box.	25 do Seed grain, 1 gal. Alcohol, 20 lbs of Soap each fam-
2 or 3 good yoke of oxen between the age of 4 and 10 years.	ily, 4 or 5 Fish hooks and lines for do.
2 or more milch cows.	15 lbs. Iron and Steel.
1 or more good beeves.	A few lbs of wrought nails,
3 sheep if they can be obtained.	One or more sets of saw
1000 lbs. of flour or other bread or bread stuffs in good sacks.	or grist mill Irons to company of 100 famil- ies,
1 good musket or rifle to each male over the age of 12 years.	2 sets of Pully Blocks and ropes to each co'y for crossing rivers,
1 lb. Powder,	1 good Seine and hook
4 do Lead,	for each company,
1 do Tea.	From 25 to 100 lbs of
5 do Coffee.	Farming & mechanical
100 do Sugar,	tools,
1 do Cayenne Pepper,	Cooking utentials to
2 do Black do,	consist of a Bake ket-
4 do Mustard,	tle, frying pan, coffee
10 do Rice for each fam- ily,	pot, & tea kettle; Tin cups, plates, knives
1 do Cinnamon,	forks, spoons, & pans
4 do Cloves,	as few as will do.
1 doz Nutmegs,	A good tent and furni-
25 lbs Salt,	ture to each 2 families.
5 do Saleratus,	Clothing & bedding to
10 do Dried apples.	each fami'y not to ex-
4 bush. of Beans.	ceed 500 pounds.
A few lbs of dried Beef or Bacon.	Ten extra teams for each company of 100 fam-
5 lbs dried Peaches,	ilies.
20 do do Pumpkin,	

N. B. In addition to the above list, horse and mule teams, can be used as well as oxen. Many items of comfort and convenience will suggust themselves to a wise and provident people, and can be laid in in' season; but none should start without filling the original bill.

Bill of Particulars showing what was to be taken in the exodus to the west in the spring of 1846. (Extract from the Nauvoo Neighbour, *29 October 1845)*

Emigrants with wagons passing through Echo Canyon.
(LDS Church History Library and Archives)

parts they already knew about hunting for food, fetching water and using it sparingly, lighting fires, mending wagons, home cure remedies — these were all second nature. On arriving at the Great Salt Lake Valley it was only just the beginning.

Those first families that emigrated would have had to find the means to pay for their own passage to America and in some cases this led to even more hardship for any family members left behind. Parents scrimped and saved to send their children over one by one, as money allowed. Farms and cottages were mortgaged to finance the voyage and often those family members who remained here found their inheritances worthless. It is easy to see how there could have been bitterness, not only had this new Church taken away their loved ones but had imposed a financial burden as well. It is not hard to understand, then, that in some cases these emigrants became family outcasts and were never spoken of to later generations. In later years it became easier to make this journey as in 1850 the Perpetual Emigration Fund Company was set up. This was created to help the poor, especially from

A Mormon encampment. (LDS Church History Library and Archives)

126

Europe, to make the move and those that it helped were expected to reimburse the fund after settlement in America to enable it to aid others. There were special P.E.F. Company agents in England who chartered ships or secured special sections on board others for the Mormon converts, these usually at low cost, whilst others in America helped with arranging the overland travel when they got there.

Members of the Holley family from Cherry Orchard Farm, Garway Hill, were some of those able to take advantage of this financial assistance. John and Anne (Cecil) Holley had seven sons out of which Charles, James and Henry all emigrated in the 1850s. Edwin, John and Amos all remained in the locality, whilst William went to live and work in

Wales. In John Price's diary of April 1849 he notes that he ordained Charles Holley as a priest. It was in 1855, when the fund was low (owing partially to a bad harvest, and also slow repayments from settlers), that in order to keep travelling costs down to a minimum, Church leader Brigham Young decided to set up 'Handcart Companies.' Over a period of five years, ten companies brought about 3,000 people to Salt Lake Valley, each company having a hundred carts. The journey that the Holleys undertook with the John A Hunt Company in 1856 was to become one of the most infamous of all the handcart treks across America. These two-wheeled wooden carts were approximately six to seven feet long, had a small box attached and were wide enough to span a narrow wagon track. Five people were assigned to each and when loaded with provisions and a few personal effects it weighed around four to five hundred pounds, needing two fit and able-bodied people to either push or pull it. Families with small children had carts with a canvas cover. Wagons transported the heavier belongings, one for each 20 handcarts. For the treks that had been undertaken by the earlier pioneers the covered wagons had provided at least some degree of comfort, with shelter from the elements and somewhere that the elderly and ill could rest on the journey. Horses, mules and sometimes milk cows were used to pull the wagons but oxen were the most popular for their sheer strength. They didn't require expensive harness like horses, just needing a wooden yoke around their neck. A person drove these animals by walking along the left side behind the lead oxen using a whip or prod to encourage them. A heavily laden wagon could cover about two miles in an hour when conditions were favourable.

James Holley (top) and Henry Holley. (Nancy Jolley)

A painting showing the journey being made with handcarts.
(LDS Museum of Church History and Art)

Although the three brothers and their families voyaged separately (James and family on the ship *Enoch Train* in 1856), when they crossed the plains to the west they were together. (Passenger lists for the *Enoch Train* show that the Parker family were also on board, later to find fame as the family of Robert LeRoy Parker, better known as the outlaw Butch Cassidy.) Records show Charles 35, stonemason; wife Mary 26; Henry 28, labourer; wife Lucy 20 and infant Lucy born *en route*; and James 31; wife Lucy Jane 21; Ann 3 and young James age 1 together in one group. Charles is down as a Captain of the Guard and James as a Captain of Ten. There were about 300 individuals and 56 wagons in the company when it began its journey from Iowa, following the Willie and Martin handcart companies. They were the last to set out that autumn and faced the winter conditions as they headed west. Cattle were lost, carts and wagons broke and to lighten the loads, goods were discarded by the wayside. Many suffered hypothermia and frostbite and amputations had to be made where necessary, without the aid of anaesthetic. The blizzards and conditions became so severe that a rescue party had to be sent out from Salt Lake. George D. Grant, who headed the rescue party, reported to President Brigham Young:

> It is not of much use for me to attempt to give a description of the situation of these people, for this you will learn from (others), but you can imagine between five and six hundred men, women and children, worn down by drawing handcarts through snow and mud; fainting by the wayside; falling, chilled by the cold, their feet bleeding and some of them bare to snow and frost. The sight is almost too much for the stoutest of us; but we go on doing all we can, not doubting nor despairing.

Early Salt Lake City, c.1860-70. Brigham Young wanted the streets to be wide enough for a wagon and team to turn around with ease. (LDS Church History Library and Archives)

At a place called Devil's Gate the rescue party unloaded the baggage from the Hunt Company wagons so that they could be used to transport those who were the weakest. There were around 1,000 emigrants in these companies and over 200 lost their lives on the journey across to the west.

Henry's wife, Lucy (Meadmore), gave birth on the journey but the baby did not survive and there are conflicting stories as to Lucy's own fate. There are no records of her, at present, having reached her destination and it is thought she may have returned to the east where she had family. We know little more of Charles' further life, but descendants of both Henry and James have returned to their roots bringing stories of the family. In 1996 a large Holley family reunion took place in Orcop village hall, with descendants coming from Wales, the Midlands, southern England as well as parts of Utah, USA.

In 1841, missionary James Palmer preached at the Eames household on Garway Hill, and before long Samuel, his wife Nancy (Castree) and their children became converts. Samuel provided for four of his children to emigrate; one of his sons, James, had already gone to America before the evangelists arrived. Their home became a welcome resting place for many of the travelling preachers. Samuel was an accomplished stonemason, learning this trade from his uncle, Samuel Watkins, with whom he had been brought up from childhood. Samuel Watkins had lived his life in Orcop and was 94 years old when he died in 1849. Young Samuel

Samuel Eames. (Jay Burrup)

129

built at least three cottages on the hill including The Shady and then later Dingle Cottage, on plots which had been allotted under the Enclosure Act. At Orcop he had been forced to leave a house uncompleted when he suffered ill health. By the census of 1851 he and wife Nancy are shown as living at the White Rocks with eldest son John and his family. His hard earned savings were used in helping to finance the passage of his other children and their families. In 1855, Nancy died and was buried in Garway churchyard. By 1861 the rest of the family had moved from the hill and were living in a rented farmhouse at Michaelchurch Escley, a few miles to the north-west. In his letters to his family in America Samuel pleaded with them to send funds to help with the passage.

'I sold all that I had and divided the money and sent four of my children to America.' My dear children, show these few lines to all my friends and to your bishop and to the high counsel and I do ask you my dear brothers and sisters in the name of God to take my case into consideration and do all you can to help me and my son and family to come out of this wicked and dark country for I cannot make myself contented to die here.

Mary Ann Eames, wife of John Carver. (Jay Burrup)

They duly succeeded in collecting enough funds and finally he, son John and his family of ten children set sail from Liverpool on 30 June 1868, on the ship *Minnesota*. They arrived in New York in July and from there began the arduous journey westward. Samuel finally fulfilled his dream of reaching the promised land and in 1869, at the age of 79, he reached Utah. However, the ordeal of such a trek proved too much for a man of his age and within two months of his arrival Samuel died. His only daughter, Mary Ann, fell in love with the missionary John Carver who hailed from Clifford on the banks of the Wye in north Herefordshire. They got married on board the ship *Josiah Bradlee* in 1850, after having stayed on board ship in port at Liverpool for a fortnight because of a raging storm. When they eventually sailed it was a rough voyage for John Carver notes in his diary how they had to be assisted to stand during their marriage ceremony. After much moving the Carvers eventually settled in Plain City, Utah, their first home a dugout, a form of dwelling described in *Plain City History, Daughters of the Utah Pioneers, Plain City Camp*:

*John Carver.
(Jay Burrup)*

The first homes were 'dugouts' as these were the quickest and easiest made in that timber-less and rock-less section. [They] had dirt floors and roofs, a fireplace in one end, and a door and a window in the other. There was no glass at first. Sagebrush was used for fuel, also for light. They were usually about 105 feet by 15 feet. It was necessary to get down steps to get into them. Some were made of sod and dirt, others were made of dirt and boards. The sod was used in the construction of the walls. The dirt floors got so hard in the summer that they could be wiped with a wet cloth. There were cupboards built in the side of the walls. By digging into the earth, steps were made level. This was where they put their dishes. A bake oven hung in the fireplace. The roofs were made by first covering them with cottonwood timbers and willows from the Weber River, then a layer of rushes and a thick layer of dirt.

Doreen Ruck and Jay Burrup. Doreen is related to the Castree family and Jay is a direct descendant of Mary Ann Eames and John Carver. He is an archivist and information specialist at the Church Office Building in Salt lake City and it was his visit to Herefordshire that led to further research into the Garway Hill emigrants

James Palmer married Mary Anne Price of The Pigeon House. (LDS Church History Library and Archives)

Later buildings were made of adobe, basically mud bricks, each 4 x 4 x 12 inches, but with the help of Henry Eames, John Carver built the very first log cabin in the settlement. John and Mary's home still stands today and has been designated as the 'Daughters of Utah Pioneers' museum.

One of the earliest Garway Hill residents to leave these shores was 27-year-old Mary Anne Price. She lived with her sister Mrs Elizabeth Knight who was housekeeper at the Pigeon House farm, the home of their uncle, farmer Daniel Price. These were relations of the Price family at New Inn, Bagwyllydiart. Mary Anne fell in love with the young, dynamic missionary, James Palmer, who had often stayed at the Price household when he was working in the area. On one of his visits he baptised Mary Anne at a selected place on the farm. He quotes in his diary: 'It was made manifest to me at this baptism and confirmation that I had baptised the person who was designed by providence to become my wife. I wrote down the following words: "And here I record that I have this day baptised a girl who will become my wife".'

In March 1842, when James completed his missionary work in the Garway area and left for America, young Mary Anne went with him. They married on 14 March at Liverpool, then the following day embarked on the *Hanover* bound for New Orleans. From there they went to Nauvoo where James' skill as a stonemason was very much in demand, with him working on the building of both the Mormon Church and also in the construction of Brigham Youngs' house. He was amongst the 50 volunteers who escorted Young and his pioneers on the first part of his journey to the west, before returning to fetch his family and set off for Missouri. They settled here for a while but the terrible conditions, with many dying from sickness and cholera, pushed them into following in Young's footsteps.

Mary never made a return journey to England to visit her family. Two of their babies died in infancy, one at Nauvoo, the other from sickness in Missouri, but baby Mary Anne, born in 1850 in Salt Lake, survived, later to marry Frederick Schoppe of Salt Lake City. They had three children.

Just a stone's throw along the road from Pigeon House farm was Middle Moors, the home of James Bevan. At 21 years old he became the first of the Garway Hill converts to emigrate when he sailed in January 1842 on board the *Hope* from Liverpool. He was the third son of John and Anne (Burford) Bevan. This family can be traced back to Evanie and Margaretta Bevan in the late 1600s, who lived in Orcop, as did the successive generations. James was one of seven children, Elizabeth being the only girl. Brothers George and Joseph also emigrated to America later on, with the intention of joining their brother, but because of the religious persecution that they faced decided to stay in the east and both settled around New York. Amos left for a new life in New Zealand, leaving William, who was a cripple, John and Elizabeth at home on the hill. We know few details of those first few years after James emigrated except that along with thousands of those first converts he settled in Nauvoo. About this time a request was made to the Mormons by the United States Army to supply fit men of fighting age to assist in the war with Mexico. The 500 strong Mormon Battalion was formed of which James was one, along with at least six other Herefordshire men. On enlistment he is described as 25 years old, 5 feet 10 inches tall, grey eyes, auburn hair and a light complexion. After receiving their arms and camp supplies they began on the long trek to Santa Fe, New Mexico. They marched around 2,000 miles on foot across a hostile environment, over rough territory where roads had to be made. Many lives were claimed through sickness and those who died were buried on the wayside. Lieutenant Colonel Cooke of the Mormon Battalion noted:

> History may be searched in vain for an equal march of infantry. Half of it has been through a wilderness, where nothing but savages and wild beasts are found, or deserts where, for want of water, there is no living creature. There, with almost hopeless labor, we have dug deep wells, which the future traveler will enjoy. Without a guide who had traversed them we have ventured into trackless tablelands where water was not found for several marches. With crowbar and pick and axe in hand, we have worked our way over mountains, which seemed to defy aught save the wild goat, and hewed a pass through a chasm of living rock more narrow than our wagons. Thus, marching half naked and half fed, and living upon wild animals, we have discovered and made a road of great value to our country.

James Bevan became part of the sick detachment of the Battalion along with those too weak or ill to keep up. They separated from the main body to spend the winter at Fort

Pueblo, Colorado, intending to travel on to California the following year. Whilst en route in the spring they discovered they were only a few days behind Brigham Young and his group heading to the west. When they arrived in Salt Lake Valley only a few days after the first settlers, they were in military order and marching to the fife and drum. Later he helped to build the old fort, which was on the site where Pioneer Square is today. In 1850 he returned to Council Bluffs, Iowa, where he married Mary Shields. They returned west and settled at Tooele, about 60 miles from Salt Lake City. Later, James took a second, polygamous wife, Isabell McPherson, who had been a friend of Mary's in Scotland. He fathered 23 children and helped to raise two others. Life was not so unlike the one he had left behind in England. Alice Bates Herron, a granddaughter, writes the following in her *History of James Bevan.*

> They were a happy family in spite of the early pioneer hardships. Their home was made of logs with a thatched roof, candles were used for light and wood for heating. Like all other early pioneers, farming was the chief occupation. A man acquired a tract of land, planted fruit trees, raised his grain for bread, had bees to supply their honey, raised cows, sheep or pigs for their meat; each family had chickens and eggs to market. Sometimes he would earn extra money by hauling logs from the hills to build new homes in the village. At times when the heavy rains came, the roof of the house would leak and the beds would be too damp to sleep in. As soon as possible the thatched roofs were replaced with tight ones made of wood. The Bevan children were kept busy in the fall of the year cutting peaches, apples and prunes for drying. Racks were built to dry the fruit on and when it was dried it was sacked and sometimes taken to Salt Lake to sell. It was a thrilling time when a family had enough fruit to sell because they could then exchange it for sewing material, sugar and other necessities, which were very scarce in those days.

Lucy Castree Crump (Sue Rice)

They also had to contend with the threat of attack from local Indian tribes and wild animals, as well as the severe winters with deep snows. Later, however, he became great friends with a Native Indian, Weiber Tom, who often visited the Bevan home and helped James with chores around the place.

James died on 26 October 1894 at the age of 73. On 30 June 2001 members of his family gathered to honour him as a Mormon Pioneer memorial marker was placed on his grave.

Members of the Castree (Castry) family from White Rocks were also amongst the very first of the converts. Philip, Richard, Elizabeth, John (the Teacher mentioned in the 1840 Minutes extract) and Lucy were all descended, down one line or another, from John Castree, born in 1778, a Chelsea Pensioner, and his wife, Hannah Booth,

Daniel Crump (Sue Rice)

from Kent. They were living in a couple of the cottages in the 'Rocks' and some meetings were held there. Lucy who married Daniel Crump, another family with a White Rocks connection, was the only one who we know emigrated. However, this was not until many years later in the 1870s and the records of their deaths show them as living in Spanish Fork, Utah. Philip, Richard and Elizabeth at various stages all got excommunicated from the Church, for transgression, but may have had subsequent baptisms. The Castrees were a colourful family: a Jeremiah, William and George all found notoriety in the *Hereford Times* with an account of an assault charge. Elizabeth made the press with an attempted suicide in a bath tub at The Globe, Garway Hill and James, who after a short 'holiday' in Pentonville Jail, left for the sunnier climate of Australia! William and George also made the move here.

What became of the Morgans from Little Garway is still somewhat vague. We know from census records that in 1841 a Mary Morgan, widow, was head of household and from Garway Tithe details that a James A. Morgan, Skenfrith, held the land. James Palmer noted in his diaries a visit to the farm in 1842: 'I returned to Garway (early March) and found some of the Saints preparing to leave.' James Morgan, Margaret, or both are possibly amongst this group. We are not sure of the exact date or who the 'Saints' were. There are later records of a Margaret Morgan of Skenfrith marrying Theodore Curtis, a well-known figure in the Mormon Church, in Nauvoo. From the few details we have, this is probably our Margaret, but more evidence is needed. In 1857, James Palmer on a trip back to England visited Walter Morgan of Little Garway and he was amongst a small congregation at a service held at the Holley household; few services were now being held. The Garway Conference which had begun in 1841 became part of the Herefordshire Conference in 1848 which was absorbed by that of Birmingham in 1869.

A William and Hannah Williams from 'Garway Hill', England have also been found mentioned in a record from America. They are possibly the people by that name, shown in the 1851 census, who were lodging with a James and Elizabeth Hill and family in a cottage on Garway Hill. Along with a Caroline Smith 'Garway Hill' they are on the passenger list for the *International* which sailed in 1853 to New Orleans. William is shown as a mason by trade.

So it goes on — Arthur, Birch, Budge, Etheridge, Evans, Goff, Green, Griffiths, Hill, James, Jones, Knight, Lebings, Lewis, Meadmore, Morgan, Perkins, Powell, Preece, Price, Pritchard, Prosser, Reed, Ruck, Sebbourn, Skidmore, Taylor, Tayson, Wathan, Watkins, Williams — just a few of the other names from Garway that have been found during research. When a whole family emigrated, who was left to tell the tale?

These are just a few fascinating insights into some of the stories, and there are many more waiting to be told. Between 1846-1869 more than 80,000 Mormon converts crossed the plains with wagons and handcarts. All those who crossed before the completion of the Transcontinental Railroad in 1869 can be classed as true Pioneers of the American West. Those men, women and children who left their homes on Garway Hill and undertook the journey of a lifetime have earned their rightful place in the history books.

Taken on Millennium morning, 1 January 2000. (Hilary Smallwood)

Mists rising from the Monnow River. (Corinne Westacot)

John Ward's ewe meets John Benjamin's lamb. (Melannie Denn)

Little Garway's girls stepping out. (Russell Whistance)

View over White Rocks towards the Skirrid. (Corinne Westacot)

Looking down on to Garway and the silo tower at Tennersfield. (Hilary Smallwood)

Kite flying with the Malvern Hills in the background. (Hilary Smallwood)

View from the trig point over to the Black Mountains. (Hilary Smallwood)

The main ascent path where it snakes past the Black Pool and the Enclosure.
(Hilary Smallwood)

Sunset at the tower. (Elaine Goddard)

Icy Black Pool. (Hilary Smallwood)

Black Pool frozen over. (Hilary Smallwood)

Ponies in the snow with the Skirrid as a backdrop. (Russell Whistance)

13   Wartime Activities and Celebrations

Wartime on the Hill

Garway Hill has a distinct summit. Unlike some hills and mountains, when you reach the top you know you are there when the view opens up before you as a complete three hundred and sixty degree panorama. The views are well worth the effort and on a clear day you can see seven counties: Herefordshire, Monmouthshire, then in the distance the Brecon Beacons and the Radnorshire hills, to the north Shropshire with the Clee Hills and further east the Malvern Hills in Worcestershire, and finally the Forest of Dean in Gloucestershire. If it is an exceptionally clear day and you know where to look it is possible that the sun may be reflecting off the Bristol Channel and, just glimpsed down the valley, the smudge on the horizon will be Somerset.

Just like May Hill in Gloucestershire with its clump of tall trees on the summit making it recognisable for many miles around, so Garway Hill also has its distinct little landmark in the form of an octagonal brick tower built on the highest point making it stand out from all the surrounding hills. A roofless structure, it is a lasting reminder of the Second World War.

In June 1941 three RAF men arrived in Garway aboard a Chevrolet radio vehicle driven by a corporal accompanied by two airmen, and proceeded to camp on Garway Hill for three weeks assessing whether or not it would be a suitable place to have a radio transmitter.

Shortly afterwards, six civilian construction workers with a large load of building materials arrived. Together with the help of Bert Gardiner, his son Leslie and using Bert's lorry, because the delivery lorry was too large to get up the narrow track, they transported the bricks, timber, cement and other materials up to the top of Garway Hill. Two of the civilian men who came from Rhayader lodged with the Gardiners at the Garway Hill Post Office, just at the bottom of the track up to the hill. Another man lodged with Mrs Whistance at Little Garway Farm. Bill Gardiner, who now lives in Clehonger, told me that he had just left school that summer and helped with the building of the brick wall. The foreman was a man from Peterchurch. Sadly, it was learned that later in the war two of these men, who had by then been called up, were killed in action.

An octagonal wooden tower was constructed to house a radio antenna. It was 25 feet high with a conical roof which had an aperture in the centre to accommodate the aerial/ transmitter, but this was never installed. It had a first floor half way up and a second floor

The two figures in the photograph looking out from the top of the tower on Garway Hill in the mid-1940s are Lilla Meadmore from Bagwylldiart and June Neal, an evacuee from London who was staying with them. The accommodation block remained for many years and was not finally demolished until the 1970s. (Doreen Ruck)

at the top with an 18-foot ladder for access. The tower was supported by eight wooden stanchions reaching down over the wall and anchored into eight concrete bases. These can still be seen today. A further eight anchor points were located inside the brick enclosure to secure the tower frame. Around this was built the seven foot-high octagonal brick wall 14 inches thick, as a defence against fire — a big hazard on bracken-clothed hills. The offset entrance was fitted with an iron gate. Encircling the wall about 40 yards out from the tower a ditch was dug as a fire break, three feet wide and 2 feet deep.

One hundred and fifty yards further down the hillside an accommodation block was built of Broadmoor Cinderford bricks with singe brick walls which were rendered. This block was divided into two rooms, one for living and one for housing instruments. Still clearly visible are two 20mm cables each of four core and eight strands projecting from the floor. Cables of this size were used to prevent a voltage reduction over a long distance and were dealing with 110 volts, direct current. This building could well have been to house a radio beam transmitter and receiver of signals. At one end was a concrete water tank to collect water from the roof. This building, which measured 21 feet by 15 feet, was also surrounded by a fire break that was just 15 yards outside the walls. A telephone cable was laid but a phone was never installed.

Even further down the hill, about 100 yards to the east of the modern radio mast and close to the boundary fence, was the engine house that was to supply the electrical energy to the tower. This was also of single brick thickness wall construction measuring 15 by 13 feet and appears to have had a corrugated asbestos roof. In here there were two diesel Lister Blackstone engines and generators, one to be used as a backup. Banks of big capacity accumulators would have been installed to store the generated electricity, each about two foot tall and nine inches square. Although the project was put on hold, the engines were regularly started up and well maintained.

The wooden tower was dismantled and removed in 1948 but for some time it had been a source of adventure for local children who climbed over the gate, gained access to the inside of the brick tower and walked precariously along the top of the walls.

This seems to be the sum total of wartime activity on the hill, except for the bomb which, I have been told, was dropped just behind Dingle Cottage in June 1941 hitting a barn belonging to Belle View. The Powell family were living at Dingle cottage and Fred Powell was employed at the Ordnance Factory at Rotherwas, near Hereford. He was working on the night shift and so his wife and young family were alone in the cottage. Other bombs fell over Orcop and Saddlebow on the same night. It would seem that a German bomber was once again looking for the Ordnance factory. The pilots knew they had to follow the river Wye and that the factory was behind Dinedor Hill. Maybe they mistook the River Monnow for the Wye and Garway Hill for Dinedor or maybe they were just getting rid of their bombs at random. Fortunately no one was hurt although a cow was killed on Saddlebow.

Celebrations on the Hill

Organised warning beacons have been lit on high positions across the country since Norman times. According to Alfred Watkins in his book *The Old Straight Track*, prehistoric man used beacons for guidance and direction; the words 'beacon' and 'beckon' have the same root and both mean 'come to me'. Many hill-top names are derived from the word beacon, for example Hereford Beacon, Trelleck Beacon and the Brecon Beacons.

All counties were required to have a military force that could be called out into action in times of emergency and the quickest way to send a message was by a system of pre-arranged fires on high points in direct sight of each other. If it was a national emergency, such as an invasion, the news could be passed with more speed than a messenger riding along difficult and dangerous roads.

At one time a tax called beaconage was levied to pay for the upkeep of the local beacon. In some lowland areas it was arranged that beacons should be lit on church towers.

By the 19th century the use of beacons as an official warning device had long passed and the lighting of bonfires on hills became a popular pastime and any excuse such as a Royal birthday, jubilees, anniversaries and military victories were all suitable excuses for a fire and a party.

Garway Hill was no exception. I am sure fires have been lit on the summit for centuries but these occasions would probably never have been recorded. In June 1897, however, occurred the Diamond Jubilee of Queen Victoria, 60 years a Queen! This called for much local organisation, the collecting of money and the putting on of events for the local people to enjoy. Many of these events were recorded in the *Hereford Times* and other local newspapers, one example being the Diamond Jubilee celebration for Kentchurch and Llangua. This took place on 22nd June 1897 at Kentchurch School where shortly after midday a 'well-provided dinner was given to the parishioners who heartily joined in the singing of the National Anthem before they sat down to dine'.

In the afternoon there was a programme of races including men's and boys bicycle races. Later in the evening a dance was held in the schoolroom, 'Miss Owen accompanying on her piano, which she lent for the occasion. Some of the people went to Garway Hill bonfire, whilst others repaired to Penlan Tump near Pontrilas. A gift of a hogshead of cider by Mr James Farr, The Elms, was much appreciated by the working- men'.

It was reported that 96 other bonfires could be seen from the top of Garway Hill and that there was also a bonfire on Coles Tump:

> On June 22nd a large bonfire was erected on Coles Tump which measured 32 yards round and 30 feet high. The timber was supplied by Mr Raymond Symonds. A number of people assembled to watch the proceedings and from this elevated position 52 other fires were seen. At 10 o'clock exactly Master Ted Symonds set fire to the stack the company singing God Save the Queen. There was soon a major blaze and at six o'clock the following evening flames were still visible.

A much grander celebration was held at the nearby Pontrilas Court on Saturday, 24 July 1897. It was described in the newspaper as 'Mr and Mrs Attwood Matthews "At Home Jubilee Cycle Sports"':

> Mr and Mrs Attwood Mathews of Pontrilas Court are never happy unless they are promoting some social function for the enjoyment and recreation of their neighbours. The weather being delightfully fine, carriages and cycles were seen approaching the residence from all directions about noon. The costly dresses of the lady cyclists, with their cycle decorations of natural and artificial flowers interweaving the revered letter of 'V.R.' called forth high approbation, and reflected the good taste of the respective owners. Luncheon and afternoon tea were provided in the dining room. The lawn was well rolled and in excellent condition for sports, the programme comprising of ten events which were gone through in a most pleasurable manner.

Pontrilas Court in the early 20th century

The events often involved the use of bicycles and comprised of a parasol ride (opening and shutting parasol), egg and spoon ride, tent pegging, threading the maze, children's ride, twist tape race, cupid's target, tortoise race and scarf ride (in couples). Most of the names of those attending would have been in a Who's Who of Herefordshire of the time.

The next Jubilee to be celebrated was that of King George V and Queen Mary in 1935. The day was Monday, 6 May and once again there was a bonfire on Garway Hill. This bonfire was well prepared and was reported in the *Hereford Times* with a photograph of the preparations and of the lighting of the bonfire that night. A feature of this bonfire was that the faggots, about 400 of them, were given by General Bate who lived at Glanmonnow in Garway. They were taken up the hill in the lorry belonging to Fred Gardiner, driven by his son, Leonard. It took two days to build the fire and the *Hereford Times* made much of the fact that this was the first lorry to have been driven to the top of Garway Hill. The organisers were obviously worried about sabotage because all Sunday night four men were on guard and were refreshed at intervals by hot tea.

The last half-century has seen beacons on Garway Hill celebrating the Queen's Silver Jubilee in 1977 and her Golden Jubilee in 2002. Beacons were lit on many hills and could be seen far into the distance. There was a very big celebration on the hill on Monday, 8 May 1995 on the 50th anniversary of the ending of World War Two in Europe, VE day. Simultaneously, at a pre-ordained time, all the beacons throughout the land were lit. It was much too early and too light and therefore they lost their impact. On Garway Hill, a very loud firework was let off to signify the start of the two minutes silence, at the end of which the beacon was lit.

*Putting the finishing touches to the beacon on Garway Hill in 1935. (*Hereford Times*)*

Another memorable occasion on the summit was on Wednesday, 11 August 1999 when at about 11am, a hundred or so people gathered to witness the rare spectacle of the total eclipse of the sun. As the appointed hour drew near the daylight faded and darkness descended with the silhouettes of the Skirrid and Sugarloaf mountains fading away, the bird song fell silent and an eerie darkness and stillness fell over the hill. Excited chatter became muted and was replaced by a tangible sense of awe. Unfortunately the cloudy weather obscured the sun apart from a brief moment as the eclipse approached. As the sky brightened there were large breaks in the cloud and people peered intently through special lenses until the shadow of the moon passed from the face of the sun.

The beacon on Garway Hill on George V's Silver Jubilee, 1935

On a bitterly cold, snowy weekend in December of 1972, soldiers of 'D Company', a Territorial Army unit based in Ross-on-Wye, were camped on the very top of the hill. A very tall aerial was erected and the soldiers were in contact with, amongst others, a similar unit camped on the Wrekin in Shropshire. This illustrates the limitations of mobile radio communications in the pre-satellite and mobile phone era.

In the late 1970s and early 1980s when the craze for CB radio (Citizens' Band Radio) was reaching its peak, it was a familiar sight to see cars parked (illegally) on the summit of the hill and out of which long aerials protruded. In the same way that the Internet chat rooms do today, CB allowed people to get to know one another in a quasi-anonymous manner. Because of recent developments such as mobile phones and the Internet, CB has lost much of its appeal. Sadly, one of these young CB enthusiasts was electrocuted when his radio aerial touched an overhead power line on Garway Hill.

Garway Hill has always been a favourite spot for model aeroplane enthusiasts with their gliders and radio-controlled aircraft.

Occasionally there has been the intrusion of motorcycles using the hill illegally for scrambling. This causes damage to the vegetation and is harmful to the stock on the hill. There are notices expressly forbidding the riding of any vehicles on the hill.

At Little Corras farm on the slopes of Garway Hill is the thriving business, Monnow Events. On the 350 acres site many adventurous activities are carried out with 'paintball war' in dense woodland, target archery and clay pigeon shooting. The quad bike trail is an exciting ride in spectacular scenery.

14　Stories and Legends

Folklore as a generic term possibly reflects the culture of an area, also its people, and includes tales, legends, oral history, proverbs, popular beliefs, customs, poetry, music and dance. Garway hill has a surprisingly rich amount of many of these components that have survived by one means or another through the centuries up to the present day.

A very popular current belief, though there is very little evidence to prove it either way, is the existence of a black cat-like beast. One such mysterious black beast was spotted prowling the south Herefordshire countryside just after a large animal supposedly attacked a young boy a few miles away in Monmouthshire. It was reported in the *Hereford Times* on 31 of August 2000 that Richard and Helen Bayley, who were on holiday, spotted a completely black animal on Garway Hill in the afternoon of the bank holiday Sunday. Mr Bayley said that they saw the animal close to the top. Mrs Bayley at first thought that it was a 'big fox' but soon realised that it was a lot bigger, darker and bolder. They reported that the creature prowled around and acted nonchalantly 200 yards away from them for roughly a minute before it disappeared in the high, dense bracken. Mr Bayley, a retired psychiatric nurse, said that the cat was bigger than anything that he had seen before with thick haunches, a large body around 3 feet long and a sleek s-shaped tail.

This sighting happened just five days after a boy called Joshua Hopkins aged 11 from Trellech was attacked by a large animal and was left with scarring across his face, which experts concluded 'was consistent with that of claw marks left by a panther type creature'.

Many other sightings have been made by local hunters who have seen large animals looking for prey in the twilight, or people spotting them early in the morning. One such sighting was made by Mr Ward, a solicitor from The White House on the hill, who reported seeing a puma-type creature playing in his garden.

Witches also feature in tales of Garway Hill. An old saying, dating back through the centuries, claims that the water on Garway Hill will run dry if nine witches are not present between Orcop and Garway Hill. Witch hunting was an evil practice carried out in the 16th and 17th centuries. Apparently, according to local beliefs, the hunting of witches took place in this area and the barbaric practice of burning women alive who were thought to be witches has been rumoured to have taken place on Garway Hill common itself, with reports of five to ten convictions over the course of time.

The main source of legend focused on Garway hill and the surrounding area, however, is that of a figure known locally as Jacky Kent. Other areas may call him Jack O'Kent, John O'Gwent or Siôn O'Kent (Siôn is Welsh equivalent for John). Along with the many names used to identify the legendary figure, various titles have been used to describe him too, although all the stories about him are similar. He was known as a cleric, a giant, a wizard, a magician and a trickster — or maybe all of these, but all of the accounts have one thing in common, that he was credited with possessing supernatural powers. Jack was said to have created many of the geological features of the area and then from these formations many of the other legends were born.

Margaret Eyer, who 1904 wrote *Folklore of The Wye Valley*, documented some of the stories, which were customary in the area. She stated: 'I can not give the names of my informants for I do not know them myself. These stories are often told in chance meetings of folk crossing a moor, by men stripping bark in the woods, women in little cottages miles away from any village and girls showing me short cuts from hill to hill'. This indicates that the stories were well known and kept close to the hearts of many of the peoples in the area even in to the early 20th century.

Many of the stories of Jacky Kent involve Satan or Old Nick, which was a layman's term for the Devil, and it was said that Jacky got his powers by selling his soul to the Devil. The deal was that Jack would possess unearthly powers and in return the Devil would take his soul when he died. But the power of Jacky Kent was his popularity, and because he was a rogue and trickster, he always got the better of 'Old Nick'.

A Garway Hill legend states that Jack O'Kent and the Devil were trying to construct a weir to make a fishpond at Orcop Hill with huge white boulders from far away, but on their way to Orcop they accidentally dropped the stones on Garway Hill. The story tells how Jack and the Devil were carrying the boulders in their aprons, jumping from hilltop to hilltop with their heavy loads, when somehow their apron strings broke at the summit of Garway hill and they both lost their gigantic cargo. The stones then bounced and rolled down the hillside and came to rest on the southern slopes. Those stones are still there to this day and are known as the White Rocks, and give the name to the hamlet found nestling here.

Jacky Kent's fondness for stones is told in other legends. One such story is that he laid a bet with the Devil that the Sugar Loaf was higher than the Malvern Hills. When Jack was proved to be right, the Devil, in a rage, tried to raise the level of the Malvern Hills by dumping an apron full of soil on their tops, but he must have used the same unreliable apron, for as he was over the Skirrid his apron strings broke again and the soil fell out forming the tump at the northern end known as 'Little Billy'. Jack was also said to be responsible for the three tall stones in the village of Trellech. The stones are set in a field close to the Monmouth to Chepstow road, standing in a line 12m (39ft) long. Jack and the devil put them there during a megalith throwing competition, he and the devil flinging the monstrous stones from the Skirrid Mountain, 14 miles away. As the Devil went to cast the fourth stone, weakened by the effort of throwing the three previous stones, his foot slipped and formed a deep hollow, leaving the gash in the side of the Skirrid. Losing his balance in the process, the fourth stone fell short of Jack's mark. Jack won the competition.

There are many stories for Jack outwitting the Devil and getting the better of him:

Jack o' Kent was a clever one, and not even the Devil could get the better of a deal with him but it wasn't for the lack of trying.

One year the Devil saw that Jack had bought a new field. He therefore proposed to Jack that they split the crop between them; Jack would plant the crop and he, the Devil, would ensure that the rain and the sun all came at the right time of year. Knowing how much damage a spell of bad weather could do, Jack was happy enough with this, and he asked the Devil which half he wanted, the part of the crop that was above or below ground? The Devil asked for the top half, thinking of fields of waving corn ripening in the sun.

So off went Jack and planted and tended his crop, whilst the Devil saw that the sun shone and the rain poured. Then came the time to harvest the crop. There was the Devil poised with his sickle sharpened specially, but he wasn't so happy when he saw the fine growth of worthless leaves that were his half of the crop, and even less so when he saw Jack digging up pound after pound of big, healthy turnips.

Come the next year the Devil proposed a similar bargain, only this time he would take the bottoms. Jack agreed and all went as in the previous year, with plentiful rain and abundant sunshine and the crop yielded bountifully. Harvest time came around again and sure enough this time Jack had planted a wheat crop so that he could have all the valuable straw and grain while the Devil was left with the useless roots.

The Devil then asked for another chance to reap a yield and get the better of Jack. This time he insisted that a wheat crop was planted. The growing season was ideal again as the Devil controlled the weather and the ears of wheat were better than ever seen before. The Devil then proposed a competition in which they would both harvest the crop with their sickles and whatever was cut was retained by that individual. As the Devil's strength was superior to that of Jack's the Devil thought that he was bound to reap most of the crop.

The competition started but soon Jack had harvested much of the field while the Devil's progress was pitifully slow as he swore at the bluntness of his sickle. Jack had nearly all of the crop harvested whilst the Devil only had a few straggly bushels. Jack celebrated his victory as the Devil left, cursing with his tail between his legs and empty handed. Unknown to the Devil, the night before the competition Jack sneaked in to the field and pushed iron knitting needles in to the ground where the devil would start. This quickly blunted the Devil's scythe making it useless and reaping impossible, so ensuring that Jack would take the lion's share of the crop.

Jack and the crows

When Jack was a young lad he worked for a farmer. One day the farmer wanted to go to the fair in a nearby town and instructed Jack to stay behind and keep the crows from destroying the crops. The farmer left Jack in the field warding off the crows, but whilst at the fair he came across Jack. Annoyed, he asked Jack what in heaven's name did he think he was doing. Jack replied that he had everything under control and that he had talked with the birds and told them to stay away from the crops. Obviously the farmer was angry and thought that he was being made a fool of. However, on their return home he was astonished to see all the crows perched on the barn roof and the crops untouched as Jack had said.

The barn where the crows were perched is said to have stood at Bagwllydiart until the 1960s and had an inscription 'I.O. Kent 1956' carved into one its beams.

The Bridge at Kentchurch

Jack was in a desperate need to cross the river Monnow at Kentchurch before nightfall, it has been said, to see a love interest! Unfortunately he found that he could not cross the river. The Devil appeared, saying that he could build a bridge in moments, but in return would have to take the soul of the first living thing to cross the bridge. The bridge was constructed swiftly, but the Devil stood on the far side grinning, knowing Jack's haste and that he would surely become the owner of Jack's soul. Time ticked by slowly whilst Jack worried about crossing a woman scorned by arriving late for his tryst. Then a passerby came walking along with his dog. Thinking quickly, Jack threw a loaf of bread across the bridge and the dog followed in pursuit. The dog was thus the first living thing to cross the bridge, but not possessing a soul again left the Devil empty handed. The sign of the nearby Bridge Inn depicts the story (see p.88).

Other legends of Jack include the tale of when Jack went to Chepstow market and bought a drove of pigs. The Devil thought that he should have his share and insisted that when they got back from driving the pigs the next day he would have all the curly tailed pigs (a supposed sign of healthy pigs) and Jack all the straight ones. So Jack drove the pigs through as many puddles, streams and mud as he could so that the tails would hang limp. The Devil became wise to this and tried magic to force the pigs to keep their tails curly. But the energy exerted by the Devil on the pigs was too much when combined with the long trip home. As they reached home the magic had worn off and all the tails were once again straight, so Jack kept the entire drove.

Jack owned a team of flying horses that he shod the wrong way around to deceive people who might want to track him. He made a gallop up the north side of Garway Hill which he used as a launch pad for his horses enabling him to fly wherever he went. Jack was once called upon to deliver a pie to the king which he took freshly made from Grosmont at daybreak and delivered it, still hot, to the king in London, for his breakfast. On the way Jack lost a garter which was said to be caught on a church steeple that he snagged when racing through the sky.

The Death of Jack O'Kent

For all of Jack's success in his dealings with the Devil, he knew there was still a chance that Old Nick would triumph in the end and walk off with his soul, as Jack was but a mortal being. Jack also knew that the devil would make his existence far from pleasant for all eternity in Hell. However the story goes that they both agreed that Jack's soul would be forfeit whether he was buried inside the church or outside it.

Wiley old Jack still had a trick up his sleeve and in his dying days he gave orders that he should be buried lying under and across the church wall, so that he would be neither inside nor outside.

And as a sign to his friends as to whether or not his soul was safe, he told them to hang up a piece of liver outside the church. A white dove and a black crow would then fight over it, and if the dove won then they would know he had escaped the devil for good. According to some the result is not known. Those few brave enough to watch after the funeral saw the dove and crow fly down as prophesied, and though at first the crow seemed to be driving the dove away, the white bird fought back and eventually triumphed.

It is unclear why Jack O'Kent has become a lesser figure in wider folklore circles as his power, abilities and legends are equal to if not better than his those who were contemporary with him. Maybe it was Jack's success at beating the Devil which didn't place him higher in the proverb-rich folk tale culture. As an individual folk figure, ambiguity has shadowed his manifestation, and Jack's existence has been a much-deliberated topic of conversation. In Alex Gibbon's *The Mystery of Jack of Kent and the Fate of Owain Glyndwr*, links were made between the Welsh chieftain who apparently settled at Kentchurch after his defeat in England, and whose daughter married into the Scudamore family who still live in Kentchurch Court to the present day. There is only one known picture of Jacky Kent which is also said to be the portrait of Owain Glyndwr.

Michael Mortimer wrote this poem:

Jack O'Kent

The fame of Jack o'Kent spread far and wide,
A mighty wizard, strong in word and deed.
'Twas said that those who crossed him always died.
For even greater power did he greed,
So off he went with Lucifer to plead.
A devlish, deadly bargain was then made
His very soul to Satan he did cede;
Whether in church or out his body laid;
His soul was lost to gain the occult power he craved.

The power of Jack o'Kent was now so great,
He challenged Satan's strength to put to test.
From Skirrid's Mount they hurled huge blocks of slate
And Jack's three stones at Trellech came to rest.
At Kentchurch too, he showed the power possessed
And cross the Monnow caused a bridge to fall.
Determined that the Devil he would best,
In death the covenant Jack did forestall;
His body laid to rest beneath Grosmont's church wall.

145

Another poem is from an 18th-century folk song that depicts the type of people who lived in this area. This is about a party which took place in Garway and which was attended by folk from neighbouring Orcop and a very unlucky and unfortunate outsider:

Gritton of Garway and the Murdered Man's Lament

I was a wrestler bold and strong as any man might be,
In England's land there was no man that could wrestle long with me,
Fair play I loved, and threw him down without an anger look,
And now in lamentation these things I sorely book.

To Garway's cruel feast I went, it was a hapless night,
I bring my God to witness I did not wish to fight,
But Orcop's men are ignorant and savage to degree,
And nothing less would do but they must have the life from me.

Two seconds they were false and pretended friendship there,
Oh, such hollow friendship I bid you all beware,
For long I was a fighting 'till I was out of breath,
When they held my hands behind me, and I was beat to death.

This poem is taken from *Orcop the Story of a Herefordshire Village from Pre-history to Present Time*, by Delphine Coleman. The people of the area were obviously not to be trifled with, and were also said to have a reputation of being very jealous of newcomers who ventured to court girls at local dances. The lament may also give an insight into that area which is not really Welsh or English but a land of their own through the quote saying 'In England's land … fair play I loved …'. But sorrowfully he found himself to be in a much more savage place.

Effigies were used as a magical symbol by superstitious people in the area possibly up until the last century to ward off evil spirits and bring better fortune. One such effigy was found as late as the 1950s on the hill which supposedly had connotations for a child born out of wedlock.

15 Management for the Future

The grassland on Garway Hill has been maintained for centuries by commoners exercising their rights to graze livestock on the common. It is hoped that this will continue well into the future.

Bracken has become very invasive on the common and it is hoped that an annual programme of cutting and bruising of bracken will reduce its vigour. This will be of benefit to grazing livestock as more open grassland becomes available. It will also be of benefit to the grasses and wildflowers making up the acid grassland community and is likely to improve the breeding success of birds such as the skylark.

The hedges bordering the common contain a variety of species such as hawthorn, blackthorn, crab apple and hazel. However, in many places the hedges have grown very tall and gappy. It is hoped that funding will be secured to restore these hedges by re-planting many of the gaps. They will then provide important wildlife corridors and supply a range of fruit and berries for a variety of bird species. Locally made bird boxes will be installed and will provide nesting places for species such as blue tits, great tits and maybe even redstarts or pied flycatchers.

Gorse will be planted around the Black Pool to provide additional cover for newts, frogs and toads. The pond at White Rocks will be cleared and over-hanging branches removed. This timber will be stacked in piles to provide habitat for the larvae of glow-worms.

In April 2007, a group of local volunteers started doing a regular butterfly transect walk on the common. This involves regularly walking the same route and recording the species of butterfly that are seen. It is hoped that this will continue each year and that a comprehensive picture of the common's butterflies will emerge.

The common has a great deal of archaeological interest. The sensitive clearance of bracken will make the archaeological features more visible and reduce the damage being caused to the archaeological fabric by the root systems of bracken.

Carefully sited interpretation panels will explain the ecology and archaeology of the common.

As well as being of considerable ecological and archaeological interest, Garway Hill is above all a place of immense value to local people. It is hoped that people will continue to enjoy exploring the many inter-connecting paths on the common and enjoy the enthralling view from the summit for very many years to come.

School visits to the common will be arranged giving local children the chance to learn about its wildlife and history. It is hoped that this will engender a sense of the beauty and value of the common that will remain with these children as they become adults and in turn become the next generation of guardians of Garway Hill.

Garway Parish Council has been the registered owner of Garway Hill common since the Commons Registration Act of 1965. It gave permission for the formation of Garway Hill Commoners Association in 2004 and has subsequently agreed to Garway Hill common being part of the Herefordshire Community Commons Project led by Herefordshire Nature Trust. In this capacity it agreed to the Higher Level Stewardship application made to Natural England in June 2007. Garway Parish Council continues to act as a responsible custodian of Garway Hill common.

Epilogue   The Perfect Hill

Hidden between the lines of this book is a barely concealed passion for a hill. The sense of time and place is very strong on Garway Hill; it forms bonds with people's souls. For the Iron Age families who lived on its eastern slope, for Lettie Cole writing verses nearly a century ago and for those who are lucky enough to live here now, Garway Hill was, and is, special. This is a unique place where lowland Herefordshire gets tempted by altitude and the wildness of Wales.

From a distance Garway Hill is unremarkable, especially when compared to the volcanic shapes of the Skirrid or the Sugarloaf. Part of its charm comes from the surprise it springs when you complete your climb. Steep enough to demand a little effort to reach the top, ascending Garway Hill lets you feel you've achieved something. There is a definite summit from which the land slopes conveniently away, giving an unbroken wraparound view, all the more remarkable for its unexpectedness. If hills take part of their character from the things they look out on, then Garway is magnified by the spectacular perspective it delivers: to the north, the grey-blue forms of the Shropshire Hills; to the east, the Malverns and the Cotswold escarpment; in the south, an occasional glimpse of the glinting Severn and in the west the first mountains of Wales. In the various seasons, at different times of day the view changes, revealing towns, villages, churches and castles that were not visible before. The hill also has its own landmarks: the Black Pool, the blue-bell woods on its western flank, the wartime signalling tower on the summit, the tumbling boulders of White Rocks and the hidden Iron Age settlement on its eastern crest.

It is small enough to get to know intimately and this is probably what binds people to the hill — a daily familiarity with its micro-universe of birds, bracken, white horses, flowers, sheep, springs, trees and rocks. It is a quiet, unspoilt, unthreatening hill, and yet, sometimes, at night or in the mists, you get a sense of its more mysterious and timeless life.

We are happy, in this book, to record its story and we are privileged to live here just a while.

Bibliography

Chapter 1   Early Settlements
Ross, Anne *The Pagan Celts*, New Edition 1980
Powell, T.G.E. *The Celts,* Thames & Hudson 1980
Webster, Graham *The Roman Imperial Army*, A&C Black 1969
Salway, Peter *Roman Britain*, OUP 1985

Chapter 2   A History of Common Land
Hoskins, W.G. & Dudley Stamp, L. *The Common Lands of England and Wales,*
    New Naturalist Series 1963
Duncumb, John *General View of Agriculture of the County of Hereford*, 1805
Woolhope Transactions, 1958 & 1961

Chapter 3   Lords of the Manor of Garway
Billière de la, General Sir Peter *Looking for Trouble*, 1994
Burkes Peerage
House of Lords Record Office, HL/PO/JO/1/352A
Manchester University John Ryland Library RYCH/3679 (Thomas Pearle)
Staffordshire Record Office D641&D1810 (Sir Wm Compton)
Herefordshire Record Office F35/RC/HI/2

Chapter 4   Archaeology
Atkinson, C. 2007a *Herefordshire Commons Survey: Garway Hill Common,*
    Herefordshire Archaeology Report 214 Hereford.
Atkinson, C. *Garway Hill Common. An Archaeological Evaluation*, Herefordshire
    Archaeological Report 214, Hereford. 2007
Fleming-Yates, Joan *The River Running By. An Historical Journey Through the Monnow
    Valley,* Wedderburn Art Ltd. 2005
Gaffney, C. & Gater, J. *Revealing the Buried Past: Geophysics for Archaeologists,*
    Tempus Publishing 2006
Gibson, A. & Woods, A. *Prehistoric Pottery for the Archaeologist,* Leicester University
    Press 1997
White, P. *The Arrow Valley Herefordshire: Archaeology, Landscape Change and
    Conservation,* Orphan Press 2003

Chapter 6   The Natural History of the Common
Bull, H.G., MD *Notes on the Birds of Herefordshire*, 1888
Horne, G. *Birds of Herefordshire*, 1898
Watkins, M.G. *Birds of a Herefordshire Parish From Temple Bar*, April 1898
Walles, C.W. and Smith, A.J. *Herefordshire Birds,* 1975

Chapter 7   Coal, Clogs and Catastrophe
Hereford and Worcester Countryside Magazine
Katie Alcock article on Kentchurch (date unknown)
Kentchurch Estate papers, Hereford Record Office
Coleman, Delphine *Orcop,* The S.P.A. Ltd 1992
Jenkins, Geraint *Traditional Country Crafts,* Routledge and Kegan Paul 1965
Linnard, William 'Woodcolliers and charcoal-burning in Wales', *Folk Life*, Vol 25, 1986

Chapter 10   The Garway Bus
Dowding, Walter *Red and White Services 1919-1949*, Red and White Services 1950
Dunabin, J.E. *The Hereford Bus,* H J Publications 1986
Greenwood, Mike & Keeley, Malcolm *The Heyday of Midland Red*, Ian Allan 2005
Kellys *Directories* for Herefordshire

Chapter 12   The Methodists and the Mormons
Larson, Carl V. *A Database of the Mormon Battalion*, 1997
Masden, Susan Arrington *I Walked to Zion*, Deseret Book Company 1994
Coleman, Delphine *Orcop,* The S.P.A. Ltd 1992
Dennis, Ronald D. *Prophet of the Jubilee*, Brigham Young University 1987
British Mormon Historical Society

Chapter 13   Wartime Activities and Celebrations
Fleming-Yates, Joan *The River Running By an Historical Journey Through the Monnow
        Valley*, Wedderburn Art 2005
Watkins, Alfred *The Old Straight Track*, 1925
Hereford Times 1897 & 1935

Chapter 14   Stories and Legends
Coleman, Delphine *Orcop,* The S.P.A Ltd 1992
Gibbon, Alex *The Mystery of Jack of Kent and the Fate of Owain Glyndwr*, Sutton
        Publishing 2004
Palmer Roy, *Herefordshire Folklore*, Logaston Press 2002

Index

The Castle Green at Hereford; A Landscape of Ritual, Royalty and Recreation
by David Whitehead

In the Dark Ages the Green was a holy place for Christians on the western edge of a country reverting to paganism. Out of this world of eddying uncertainties emerged a royal monastery, whose inmates became caretakers of a famous graveyard, given new lustre by the burial of two English royal saints – St. Guthlac and St. Ethelbert. When the latter became the patron saint of the newly established Mercian cathedral in *c.*800, the importance of the minster on Castle Green faltered but was quickly rejuvenated by the presence of a royal hall. After the Norman Conquest, the church on the Green found itself engulfed by what became a royal castle which achieved its apogee as a fortress/palace in the reign of Henry III. The story continues with the decline and neglect of the castle, punctuated occasionally with promises of restoration — and renewed use in the Civil War. For a decade or so thereafter Castle Green became a shadow-land, occupied by paupers, squatters, dualists and vandals who carried away the remaining fabric. Gradually, the local community realised that it had an asset here, rather than a liability and it later became one of England's first inner city parks.

Paperback, 136pp with over 100 black and white and 16 colour photographs.
ISBN: 978 1904396 77 2   PRICE: £12.95

Herefordshire Bricks & Brickmakers
by Edwin Davey & Rebecca Roseff

This book gives a background to the brick industry in Herefordshire, locates and explains many of those groups of hollows and ponds in the ground as old brickworks; looks at the changing sizes of bricks, the move from hand-made clamp-fired bricks to industrial production, the patterns of brickwork used and at the lives of the workers and where they lived. The last half of the book is a gazetteer of the sites of known brickworks in the county on a parish by parish basis.

Paperback, 160pp with 70 black and white and 25 colour illustrations
ISBN: 978 1904396 70 3   PRICE: £9.95

Also from Logaston Press

RAF Madley
by Fiona Macklin

The site for RAF Madley Radio School was acquired at the end of 1940 in response to a need for training bases away from the threat of German bombers. Entering operation whilst still under construction the 3.5 square mile site, one of the largest RAF bases in Britain, was soon providing training for both Ground and Air crew. The main courses were in Morse and Wireless operation, in flight practice being carried out in Dominie and Proctor aircraft. This book also tells of the sports and entertainments held on the base, its interaction with the local community and that of Hereford, of some of the personalities and pranks, of life at the base in general. It also provides a brief history of what happened to it since it closed as an RAF Radio School in 1946. Likewise the brief passage of its most infamous visitor, Rudolf Hess, is included.

Paperback, 88 pages with 45 black and white photographs.
ISBN 978 1904396 65 9   PRICE £4.95

Flying for Fun in the southern Marches
by Tony Hobbs

This book looks at the early history of manned flight in the southern Marches, from ballooning, through gliding and parachuting to flying. In doing so it considers the question as to whether the earliest manned flight in Britain was actually made in Shropshire; abortive attempts at flying in Ross; the contribution to ballooning made by Charles Rolls; the unscheduled stops of early aircraft in fields around the counties, and an individual who helped in the testing of parachutes.

More recent claims to fame and activities are also detailed, setting out the development of hang gliding, paragliding, microlight flying, and helicopter and flying enterprises in the area. Each of these activities Tony Hobbs also attempts in his own right in the spirit of the early pioneers, meeting today's enthusiasts in the hope it may encourage others to also 'have a go' — though, in at least one case, with less self harm resulting!

Paperback, 128pp, 75 black and white illustrations.
ISBN 978 1904396 79 6   PRICE: £9.95

Also from Logaston Press

John Venn and the Friends of the Hereford Poor
by Jean O'Donnell

The Rev. John Venn came from a circle that included William Wilberforce and trained to became an Anglican priest, moving to Hereford in 1833. Part of his parish included the area of St Owen's, one of the poorest parts of the city. Imbued with the belief that all poverty could be dispelled by work, he helped establish the Society for Aiding the Industrious. The Society soon created a hive of activity in Hereford. They built and ran a steam corn mill that milled corn at a cheaper rate than was charged elsewhere, and yet still made handsome profits which were ploughed back into other Society activities: a baths complex and subsequent swimming pool; allotments; a model farm and gardens; a coal store; a soup kitchen; and an office which also handled grants and loans. In effect, Venn created a whole mixed welfare system for the poor of Hereford.

Paperback, 144pp with 80 black and white illustrations
ISBN: 978 1904396 71 0   PRICE: £9.95

The Celtic Christian Sites
of the central and southern Marches
by John and Sarah Zaluckyj

Introductory chapters detail the arrival of Christianity in Britain and give some background to its early nature and style. The pervading philosophy behind what became the Celtic brand of Christianity is discussed: the early house monasteries of wealthy sons, the development of isolated monastic communities, the role of bishops and abbots, the nature of Christian teaching, ending with biographical details of the most important saints who had contact with the area covered. In amongst this the nature of a 'llan' is described, as are the features often considered to indicate early Christian sites — holy wells, yews, circular and /or raised churchyard enclosures, and the Christianization of pagan sites. This sets the scene for looking at 168 sites on the gazetteer that are spread across Montgomeryshire, Radnorshire, Breconshire, western Herefordshire and Gwent.

Paperback, 448pp with over 200 black and white photographs
ISBN: 1 904396 57 7   PRICE: £12.95

166